AMOK

AMOK
Nadine Fecht

KUNSTHALLE
MANNHEIM

DISTANZ

Table of content Inhaltsverzeichnis

AM

ok

Vorwort

Unter dem Titel *AMOK* zeigt die Kunsthalle Mannheim Werke der Berliner Künstlerin Nadine Fecht (*1976 in Mannheim). Sie steht für eine der vielversprechendsten zeitgenössischen Positionen im Bereich der Zeichnung und Konzeptkunst. Zentral für Nadine Fechts Arbeiten ist der Materialbegriff, der die konzeptuellen und assoziativen Bedeutungszusammenhänge des verwendeten Materials stets einbezieht bzw. diese an den Anfang stellt. Dabei lotet Fecht die Grenzen des Machbaren aus. Sei es, dass sie mit einem Bündel aus bis zu 1805 Kugelschreibern zeichnet und damit ein Werkzeug verwendet, das sie nicht mehr vollständig beherrschen kann, oder dass sie sich selbst gestellten „Schreibaufgaben" unterwirft, bei denen sie die fast endlosen Wiederholungen geschriebener Sätze an die Grenzen der psychischen sowie physischen Belastbarkeit bringen. Damit geht eine unumgängliche Selbstbefragung einher, in der sie sich mit ihrer Rolle in der Gesellschaft, mit Erwartungen und mit Selbstdisziplinierung konfrontiert.

Nadine Fecht arbeitet als Konzeptkünstlerin mit den Medien Zeichnung, Sprache, Schrift, Klang und Video. Dabei steht immer auch die Einbeziehung der Betrachterinnen und Betrachter im Vordergrund.

Die Stärke ihrer Arbeiten liegt darin, dass die in einer sehr individuellen Selbstbefragung aufgeworfenen Inhalte gleichzeitig eine große Allgemeingültigkeit haben, der sich die Betrachtenden nicht entziehen können. Doch überall, wo man glaubt, eine Antwort zu finden, tun sich neue Fragen auf. Gewohnte Sichtweisen, Begriffe, gesellschaftliche Zusammenhänge und Zuordnungen werden hinterfragt. Nadine Fecht verfremdet Kontexte, Bedeutungen und löst ein breites Spektrum an Assoziationen aus.

Immer sind es Spannungsfelder, die unaufgelöst fixiert werden und deren Pole den Bereichen der sozialen Ökonomie (wie bei der Zeichnung *Jedes Kollektiv braucht eine Richtung*), der gesellschaftlichen Rollenzuschreibung und der Selbstermächtigung eines Individuums entstammen.

In zahlreichen Arbeiten verwendet Nadine Fecht Sprache derart, dass sie tradierte und im Gebrauch gesellschaftlich festgesetzte Wortbedeutungen hinterfragt. Durch Sprache entmaterialisiert sich Kunst und wandert als Gedankenpotenzial in die Köpfe der Betrachtenden.

So steht der Titel der Ausstellung *AMOK* für Irritation und für ein offenes Nebeneinander und die mögliche Gleichzeitigkeit völliger Selbstdisziplinierung und gezielter Enthemmung. Negativ konnotiert weckt er unweigerlich die Aufmerksamkeit des Publikums.

Zahlreiche Werke der Künstlerin haben bereits Eingang in bedeutende öffentliche Sammlungen gefunden. Die Kunsthalle Mannheim freut sich, repräsentative Werke der Künstlerin in ihrer ersten musealen Einzelausstellung vorstellen zu können.

Foreword

Under the title *AMOK*, the Kunsthalle Mannheim presents the work of the Berlin-based artist Nadine Fecht (born in Mannheim in 1976). She represents one of the most promising contemporary positions in the field of drawing and concept art. The idea of the material is central to Nadine Fecht's work, which always integrates the conceptual and associative meanings of the material used, i.e. places these at the beginning of every work. In the process Fecht sounds out the limits of the possible, whether this be with a bundle of up to 1,805 ballpoint pens, a tool which she can no longer completely control, or self-imposed "writing assignments" in which the almost endless repetition of written sentences bring her to the limits of both psychological and physical endurance. This is accompanied by an inevitable self-questioning in which she confronts herself with her role in society, with expectations, and the act of self-disciplining.

Nadine Fecht is a concept artist who works with the media of drawing, language, script, sound, and video, whereby the involvement of the viewer is always in the foreground.

The strength of her work is to be found in the fact that the content, thrown up by her highly individual self-questioning, simultaneously possesses great universality, which the viewers cannot escape. However, everywhere one believes one has found an answer, new questions emerge. Habitual perspectives, concepts, social connections, and classifications are questioned. Nadine Fecht defamiliarizes contexts, meanings, thus triggering a broad spectrum of associations.

It is always moments of tension that are fixed, without being resolved, and whose opposing poles originate from the fields of social economy (as in the case of the drawing *Jedes Kollektiv braucht eine Richtung*), society's assignment of roles, and the self-empowerment of the individual.

In numerous works Nadine Fecht employs language in such a fashion that traditional meanings and those established through social use are questioned. Art becomes dematerialized through language and inscribes itself in viewers' heads as thought potential.

Thus the title of the exhibition, *AMOK*, stands for irritation and an open coexistence and potential simultaneity of complete self-discipline and concerted disinhibition. Connoted negatively, it inevitably awakens the interest of the public.

Numerous of the artist's works have already found their way into important private and public collections. The Kunsthalle Mannheim is delighted to present a selection of the artist's representative works in her first solo exhibition in a museum context.

The idea for this exhibition was developed by Thomas Köllhofer, who has curated it together with Nadine Fecht. We would like to express our special thanks to both of them, in particular the artist, for the realization of this project as well as the accompanying catalogue. Neither of them would have been possible without the generous support of the Academy of the Arts Berlin, the VG Bild-Kunst, and the LBBW Foundation. Our heartfelt thanks goes to these institutions. We would also like to thank the authors Krisztina Hunya and Kolja Reichert for their text contributions, and Colin Shepherd for his translations. Our thanks goes to Studio Pandan, in particular Ann Richter, for the design of the exceptional catalogue published by Distanz Verlag.

Die Idee zu dieser Ausstellung hatte Thomas Köllhofer, der sie gemeinsam mit Nadine Fecht kuratiert hat. Ihnen beiden, aber insbesondere der Künstlerin gilt unser außerordentlicher Dank für die Realisierung dieses Projektes sowie des begleitenden Kataloges. Beides hätte nicht realisiert werden können ohne die großzügige Unterstützung der Akademie der Künste Berlin, von VG Bild-Kunst und der LBBW-Stiftung. Dafür sei herzlich Dank gesagt. Besonderer Dank geht an die Autoren Krisztina Hunya und Kolja Reichert für ihre Textbeiträge sowie an Colin Shepherd für die Übersetzung. Studio Pandan, insbesondere Ann Richter, danken wir für die Gestaltung des im Distanz Verlag erscheinenden Kataloges.

Inge Herold

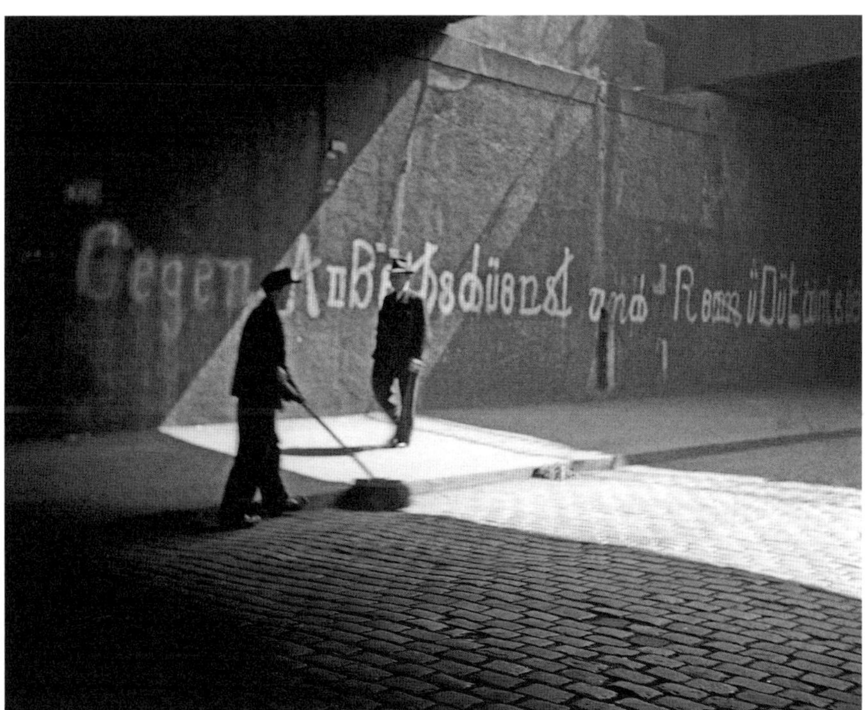

Die 1937 in Essen unübersehbar angebrachte Parole „Gegen Arbeitsdienst und Remilitarisierung" ließ sich nicht ohne Weiteres entfernen. Also suchte man sie durch Verfremdung unkenntlich zu machen. (Bild und Bildunterschrift aus Peter Longerich „Hitler", S. 475)

The slogan "Against Labor Service and Remilitarization", written in a prominent place in Essen in 1937 could not be removed. Therefore an attempt was made to make it illegible by defamiliarization. (Picture and caption from Peter Longerich "Hitler", p. 475)

A g è

macy

At the Limit

Am Limit

Thomas Köllhofer

Melancholia (detail) 2015/16

Melancholia

Using red ink Nadine Fecht incessantly writes the following sentence on a wall-sized sheet of paper measuring 271 × 555 cm: "I'm feeling blue I'm feeling blue I'm feeling blue...". At the end of a long line the sentence immediately continues onto the next, thus creating an endless text from the same statement. Fecht's use of red ink appears contradictory, but only with respect to a literal reading of the sentence, for in terms of content, and depending on the context, it means something like "I am sad / I am depressed / I am in a bad mood". The color red, especially in its direct connection with the handwriting, can be understood as an expression of emotionality, as inner involvement, while nevertheless remaining a disruptive factor. However, in the context of the creation of a work of art, the named color blue evokes the blue flower, the site of projection for romantic longing. At the same time blue corresponds to the emotional state of melancholy, which is considered a precondition, or at least one of the possibilities, for creative work.

In exhibitions Fecht displays these monumental drawings either resting against a low pedestal or, in landscape format, hanging on the wall, so that the viewer can only decipher the text by lowering their head or tilting it lightly to the side. The compulsion to read the written is very pronounced amongst the majority of people. However, in this case, after just a few lines, and on casting one's gaze over the paper, it quickly becomes apparent that nothing else is written on any other part of the paper apart from the same sentence, over and over again: "I'm feeling blue". At the beginning of every sentence the artistic "I" manifests itself, whose mood is then defined as "blue". The text structure is inscribed on the paper like a continually updated self-assurance, which ultimately no longer needs to be deciphered word for word as the lexical content is clear. In any case, due to the minute size of the characters relative to the monumental format, it is only possible to focus one's gaze on part of a line and perhaps a few letters at close range. The surroundings become blurred and elude the concentrated reading. Thus the viewer straightens up, i. e. steps further and further back in order to gain an overview of the planar expanse of the script, which, with the minimalist alterations in its red shades, unfurls like a vast plain. However, due to the fact that reading has now become superfluous, the eyes relax, the concentrated fixation changes to a dreaming gaze, which meanders, following the subtle variations of the basic motif composed of concentrations or dispersions in the script and the lines—an ideal condition providing room for thought, allowing the ever-repeated sentence "I am feeling blue" to exercise a deeper influence. The sentence has long since become embedded in the memory, and thus becomes, comparable to looking at one of the sequence of glasses from Peter

Melancholia

Mit roter Tusche schreibt Nadine Fecht auf ein wandgroßes Blatt von 271 × 555 cm ohne Unterlass den Satz: „I'm feeling blue I'm feeling blue I'm feeling blue...". Am Ende einer langen Zeile laufen die Sätze direkt weiter in die jeweils folgende, sodass ein endloser Text aus immer derselben Feststellung entsteht. Dass Fecht dafür rote Tinte verwendet, erscheint als Widerspruch, der aber nur in der wörtlichen Lesart entsteht, denn inhaltlich bedeutet der Satz je nach Zusammenhang so etwas wie „Ich bin traurig / Ich bin niedergeschlagen / Ich habe schlechte Laune". Die Farbe Rot kann insbesondere in der unmittelbaren Verbindung mit der Handschrift als Ausdruck der Emotionalität, der inneren Beteiligung verstanden werden, bleibt aber als Störfaktor bestehen. Im Kontext der Entstehung eines Kunstwerkes verweist die benannte Farbe Blau dagegen auf die blaue Blume, den Projektionsort romantischer Sehnsucht. Zugleich entspricht Blau dem Gemütszustand der Melancholie, die als Voraussetzung oder zumindest als eine der Möglichkeiten schöpferischen Arbeitens gilt.

In Ausstellungen präsentiert Fecht diese monumentale Zeichnung entweder auf einem niedrigen Sockel liegend oder als Querformat an der Wand hängend, sodass die Betrachtenden den Text nur mit gesenktem oder leicht seitlich geneigtem Kopf entziffern können. Das Bedürfnis, Geschriebenes zu lesen, ist bei den meisten Menschen sehr ausgeprägt. Hier allerdings wird nach wenigen Zeilen und beim weiteren Schweifen des Blicks über das Blatt schnell deutlich, dass nirgendwo etwas anderes steht, als immer und immer wieder derselbe Satz: „I'm feeling blue". Zu Beginn eines jeden Satzes manifestiert sich das künstlerische „Ich", dessen Stimmungslage dann als „blue" definiert wird. Wie eine sich fortschreibende Selbstvergewisserung ist das Textgefüge auf das Blatt gezeichnet, das schließlich nicht mehr Wort für Wort entziffert werden muss, da der lexikalische Inhalt offenkundig ist. Aufgrund der im Verhältnis zum monumentalen Format winzigen Schriftgröße können sowieso nur wenige Worte, nur ein Teil einer Zeile und vielleicht einige wenige Buchstaben in nächster Nähe auf einen Blick fokussiert werden. Das Umfeld verschwimmt und entzieht sich der lesenden Aufmerksamkeit. So richten sich die Betrachtenden auf, beziehungsweise treten mehr und mehr zurück, um die flächenhafte Ausdehnung des Schriftbildes überblicken zu können, das sich mit den minimalistischen Veränderungen seiner Rotschattierungen wie eine weite, landschaftliche Ebene ausbreitet. Dadurch aber, dass das Lesen überflüssig geworden ist, entspannen die Augen, verändert sich das konzentrierte Fixieren in ein träumendes Schauen, das mäandernd den subtilen Variationen des Grundmotivs folgt, die aus Verdichtungen oder Spreizungen der Schriftzüge und der Zeilen entstehen – ein idealer Zustand, um Gedanken Raum zu geben, um den immergleichen Satz „I am feeling blue" auch in der Tiefe wirksam werden zu lassen. Der Satz hat sich längst im Gedächtnis festgesetzt und so wird, vergleichbar der Betrachtung einer der

Gläserserien von Peter Drehers Reihe *Tag um Tag guter Tag*, das Nachdenken über den Inhalt ebenso fesselnd wie das Betrachten der Zeichnung selbst.

Faszinierend ist die Vorstellung der immensen skripturalen Arbeit. Wenige Tätigkeiten versinnbildlichen den Fluss der Zeit so anschaulich wie das Schreiben. Es ist eine lineare Handlung, bei der die Feder ein Äquivalent zur Zeit selbst entstehen lässt, gleich dem von der Schicksalsgöttin, der Parze Nona, gesponnenen Lebensfaden. Im Lesen wird dieser Zeitfluss mit- und nachvollzogen. Bei *Melancholia* allerdings entziehen sich die Betrachtenden dieser Gleichzeitigkeit, da sie dem Text nicht Zeile für Zeile folgen. Sie lesen den Text nur ansatzweise, haben den sich wiederholenden Inhalt erfasst, um das Blatt dann großflächig zu überblicken. Auch die repetitive Gleichmäßigkeit der Schrift regt nicht zum fokussierenden Schauen an. Abgesehen davon hat Fechts Schriftbild nichts mit der optisch wirkungsstarken Kunst der Kalligrafie gemein, da es einem gleichmäßigen und ruhigen Duktus folgt. Man ahnt das hohe Maß an Kontrolle und Konzentration, das nötig ist, um sich nicht zu verschreiben, um keine fallenden Linien zu produzieren, um mit den Schriftzügen nicht größer oder kleiner zu werden.

Nadine Fechts Schriftzeichnungen lösen zahlreiche Assoziationen aus. Sie erinnern an den monotonen Klang gesungener Mantren, das murmelnde Beten von Rosenkränzen, aber auch an manische Handlungen, wobei ihre Arbeiten eine vorab festgelegte Form, einen exakt definierten Anfang und ein gesetztes Ende haben und sich somit der Zwanghaftigkeit entziehen. Die Entstehung von Fechts Schriftzeichnungen erinnert darüber hinaus an das Schreiben der Tora und anderer religiöser Texte im Judentum durch einen Sofer STaM genannten Schreiber. Dieser bittet Gott vor jeder Schreibsitzung darum, dass er ihm genügend physische und geistige Kraft gebe, damit er die Sitzung fehlerfrei bestehe. Denn macht er auch nur einen Fehler, so muss er von vorne anfangen. Nadine Fecht muss sich einem vergleichbaren Gesetz unterworfen haben. Ihre Sätze sind fehlerfrei. Es gibt nur eine mehrfach auftretende, bewusste Veränderung in der Schreibweise von „I'm feeling blue" zu „I am feeling blue", die dann aber jeweils über eine längere Strecke – über ein Tagwerk? – gehalten wird. Da Fechts Textzeichnungen, wie auch die Tora, handgeschrieben und nicht gedruckt sind, variieren Buchstaben, Worte oder Zeilenfall sowie beschriebene und unbeschriebene Stellen. Dadurch entsteht eine schwebende Spannung, die einen wesentlichen Teil des Reizes ihrer Schriftzeichnungen ausmachen. In der fortwährenden, minimal variierenden Wiederholung spiegelt sich ein optisches Grundprinzip allen Lebens. Keine Minute, keine Stunde, kein Tag sind wie die anderen. In den Zeichnungen ist aber auch die Tagesform erkennbar, die in der Struktur von Buchstaben und Zeilenfall sichtbar ihre Spuren hinterlässt. Mit ihren minimalistischen Veränderungen des Farbklangs gleicht Fechts Zeichnung *Melancholia* einer offen daliegenden Seelenlandschaft. Tatsächlich aber wird die emotionale Spannung zwischen der Aussage „I'm feeling blue" und der gezeichneten Landschaft auf die Betrachtenden übertragen.

Dreher's series *Tag um Tag guter Tag*, where thinking about the content is as captivating as viewing the drawing itself.

The idea of the immense scribal work is fascinating. Few activities symbolize the flow of time so graphically as writing. It is a linear activity in which the pen generates an equivalent to time itself, like the thread of life spun by the god of destiny, the Parcae Nona. In the act of reading this flow of time is traced and re-enacted. However, in the case of *Melancholia* this simultaneity eludes the viewer as they do not follow the text line for line. They only read the text fleetingly, and having grasped the repeated content, they then take in the sheet as a whole, on the larger scale. The repetitive uniformity of the script also discourages focused looking. Apart from this, Fecht's handwriting has nothing in common with the optically impactful art of calligraphy, instead it follows a uniform and steady cadence. One can sense the high degree of control and concentration that is needed to avoid making mistakes, in order to prevent falling lines, in order to prevent the characters from becoming bigger or smaller.

Nadine Fecht's script drawings awaken numerous associations. They are reminiscent of the monotonous sound of sung mantras, the murmuring prayer of rosaries, or manic activities, although her works have a predetermined form, a precisely defined beginning and a composed end, and thus are free of the compulsive. Furthermore, the production of Fecht's script drawings is reminiscent of the writing of the Tora and other Jewish religious texts by a scribe known as a Sofer STaM. Before each writing session the scribe calls on God to grant him sufficient physical and spiritual energy to complete the session without making any errors—for even if he only made one mistake he would have to start from the beginning again. Nadine Fecht must have subordinated herself to a similar law. Her sentences are free of mistakes. The only irregularity is a conscious change in the spelling, which recurs numerous times, from "I'm feeling blue", to "I am feeling blue", which is then maintained over a long stretch—over a day's work? As Fecht's text drawings (like the Tora) are hand written and not printed, letters, words or the alignment, as well as written and unwritten sections, vary. This results in a floating tension which lends her script drawings a great deal of their allure. The continual repetitions with their minimal variations reflect a basic optical principle of all life. No minute, no hour, no day is like the other. However, the drawings also display her daily form, which has left visible traces in the structure of the letters and the typographical alignment. With its minimalist changes in color tone Fecht's drawing *Melancholia* resembles the open expanse of a soulscape. However, in point of fact the emotional tension between the statement "I'm feeling blue" and the drawn landscape is transferred to the viewer.

Fecht's script drawings remind one of Hanne Darboven's working method, which fixes in writing both her own lifetime as well as historical time

periods which, in some cases, she has not experienced, employing its own system and set of rules. Darboven "visualizes the concrete existence of time; her entire work is her own contemporary history: a process of living, working, perceiving as a multidimensional visualization sequence".[1] While Darboven books the writing performed in each case as the product of a day's work, Fecht questions social value systems such as discipline and self-optimization.

In addition to *Melancholia*, Nadine Fecht has created a whole series of further script drawings, which, with respect to the multiple handwritten repetitions of one and the same statement are comparable, although formally and substantively each of them express a fundamentally different approach.

hysteria

In *hysteria* Fecht writes the sentence "I AM NOT HYSTERICAL", employing large capital letters, in an apparently endless sequence on five, over two meter high sheets of paper. In contrast to *Melancholia*, the artist begins every line with the start of the sentence and takes care that the end of the line closes with the end of the sentence, as in full justification. The "I", placing itself in the world—the "I AM" providing reassurance of its own existence—forms the starting point for each line as well as every following statement. However, this time it is followed by the vehement negation "I AM NOT", only to state more emphatically what this I is not, namely "I AM NOT HYSTERICAL".

In contrast to *Melancholia* where the sentences are written like a chain of pearls, without full stop or comma, here a full stop turns every individual sentence into a closed entity, an unequivocal statement which becomes increasingly insistent as a result of the continual repetition, and which can ultimately be understood as apotropaic. At the same time the title of the work *hysteria* opens up a field of associations in which the repetitive activity can clearly be understood as manic, as "hysterical". The unambiguousness of the resolutely formulated statement appears to lose its persuasiveness—or, conversely, does the acceptance of a phenomenon, previously described as "hysterical" in the sense of an illness, resonate here?

Extending into the 20th century, hysteria was a typical clinical picture for psychological disturbances and illnesses of the female sex as diagnosed by a medical science exclusively shaped by men, i.e. hysteria was an illness imputed to women. According to its literal meaning, the word, "hysteria" means a "wandering uterus", which since antiquity was considered the cause for conspicuous psychological behavior and ultimately understood as a clinical picture indicating that women suffering from hysteria had a neurotic disturbance, which, amongst other

1 Tilman Osterwold, Hann Darboven: Zeit und Weltansichten. In: hanne darboven. Ifa exhibition catalogue. Stuttgart 2000, p. 6

Fechts Schriftzeichnungen lassen an die Arbeitsweise von Hanne Darboven denken, die sowohl eigene Lebenszeiten wie auch historische, von ihr teilweise nicht erlebte Zeiträume nach eigener Systematik und Regelhaftigkeit schreibend festgehalten hat. Darboven „visualisiert die konkrete Existenz von Zeit; ihr gesamtes Werk ist ihre eigene Zeitgeschichte: ein Prozess des Lebens, Arbeitens, Erkennens als ein mehrdimensionaler Visualisierungsablauf"[1]. Während Darboven die jeweils geleistete Schreibarbeit als Tagwerk, als vollbrachte Leistung verbucht, hinterfragt Fecht gesellschaftliche Wertesysteme wie Disziplin oder Selbstoptimierung.

Neben *Melancholia* hat Nadine Fecht eine ganze Reihe weiterer Schriftzeichnungen geschaffen, die strukturell in der vielfachen handschriftlichen Wiederholung ein und derselben Aussage durchaus vergleichbar sind, formal wie inhaltlich aber jeweils eine grundsätzlich andere Ausrichtung haben.

hysteria

Bei *hysteria* schreibt Fecht auf fünf, über zwei Meter hohen Blättern in großen Druckbuchstaben und scheinbar endloser Folge den Satz „I AM NOT HYSTERICAL". Im Gegensatz zu *Melancholia* startet die Künstlerin den Anfang jeder Zeile mit dem Beginn des Satzes und achtet darauf, dass sie am Ende der Zeile mit dem Schluss des Satzes blocksatzartig abschließt. Das sich selbst in die Welt setzende „Ich" („I") – das sich seiner eigenen Existenz vergewissernde „Ich bin" („I AM") – bildet jedes Mal den Ausgangspunkt der Zeile sowie jeder folgenden Äußerung. Diesmal folgt jedoch die vehemente Verneinung „ICH BIN NICHT" („I AM NOT"), allerdings nur, um desto nachdrücklicher zu präzisieren, was dieses Ich nicht ist, nämlich „ICH BIN NICHT HYSTERISCH." („I AM NOT HYSTERICAL.").

Im Gegensatz zu *Melancholia*, wo die Sätze wie an einer Perlenschnur ohne Punkt und Komma durchgeschrieben sind, macht hier ein Punkt jeden einzelnen Satz zu einer geschlossenen Einheit, einer unmissverständlichen, durch die ständige Wiederholung zusehends eindringlichen Aussage, die schließlich geradezu als apotropäisch verstanden werden kann. Gleichzeitig öffnet der Titel der Arbeit *hysteria* ein Assoziationsfeld, in dem repetitives Tun durchaus als manisch, als „hysterisch" verstanden werden könnte. Die Eindeutigkeit der so entschieden formulierten Aussage scheint ihre Überzeugungskraft zu verlieren – oder schwingt, gerade umgekehrt, eine Akzeptanz der früher im Sinne einer Krankheit als „hysterisch" beschriebenen Phänomene mit?

Hysterie wurde noch bis ins 20. Jahrhundert als gängiges Krankheitsbild für psychische Leiden und Erkrankungen des weiblichen Geschlechts von einer allein von Männern geprägten Medizin diagnostiziert bzw. Frauen als Erkrankung angedichtet. Dem Wortsinn nach bezeichnet „Hysteria" eine „(wandernde) Gebärmutter", die seit der Antike als Ursache für psychisch auffälliges Verhalten galt und

1 Tilman Osterwold, Hanne Darboven: Zeit und Weltansichten. In: Hanne Darboven. Ausstellungskatalog des ifa. Stuttgart 2000, S. 6

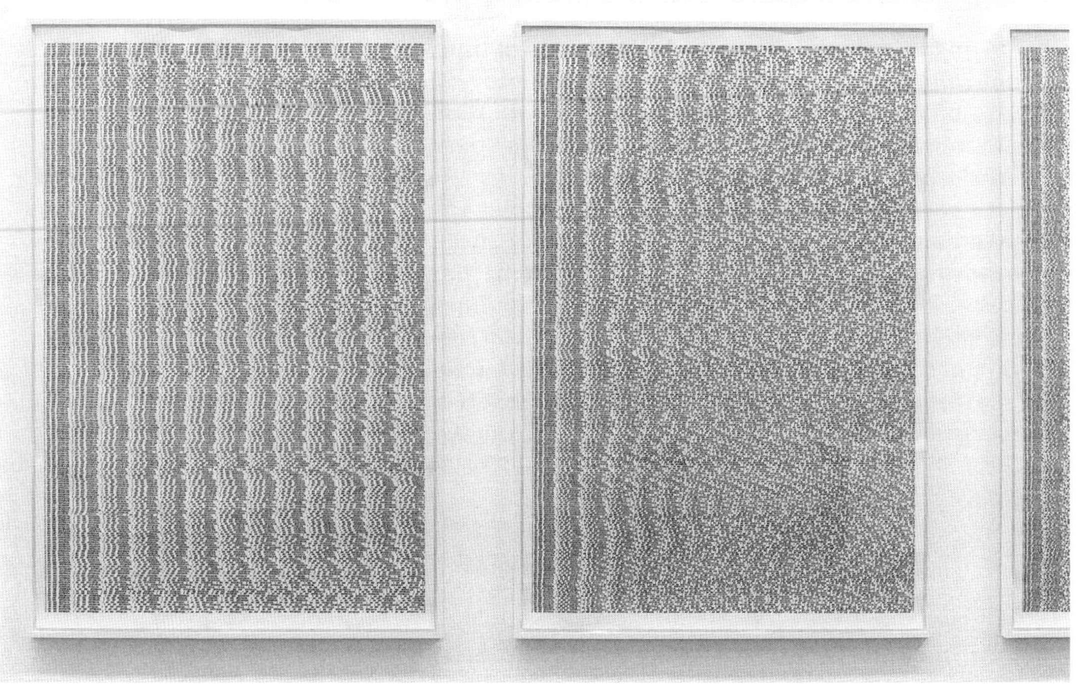

hysteria 2016 (Ausstellungsansicht **exhibition view**)

schließlich als Krankheitsbild so verstanden wurde, dass unter Hysterie leidende Frauen eine neurotische Störung hätten, die unter anderem mit oberflächlicher, labiler Affektivität und einem hohen Bedürfnis nach Geltung und Anerkennung einhergehe.[2] Indem Nadine Fecht „I AM NOT HYSTERICAL." in scheinbar unendlicher Wiederholung niederschreibt entsteht der Eindruck, sie müsse gegen etwas ihr als Frau Eingeprägtes anschreiben, so, als ob sie gerade in dem, was sie tut, beweisen wolle, dass das, was sie abwehrend schreibt, seine Richtigkeit hat bzw. dass die gegenteilige Behauptung falsch ist. Denn bis heute schwingt, wenn der Begriff „Hysterie" verwendet wird, die Vorstellung von einer als krankhaft betrachteten, weiblichen Verhaltensweise mit, die als fehlende Selbstkontrolle, mangelnde Disziplin und einer daraus folgenden ausschweifenden Emotion bis hin zu sexueller Zügellosigkeit interpretiert wird.

Auf fünf groß dimensionierten Blättern mit je rund 240 Zeilen wieder und wieder in derselben Wortfolge ein und denselben Satz zu schreiben, ist ein Projekt, dessen Durchführung nur einer höchst disziplinierten und selbstkontrollierten Person gelingen kann. Umso mehr fallen die kleinen, durch das handschriftliche Schreiben entstandenen arrhythmischen Verschiebungen von Buchstaben und Wörtern auf, die das strenge Satzgerüst von links nach rechts, also in Schreibrichtung zunehmend, in ein strukturelles Flirren versetzen. Selbst eine kontrollierte Handschrift ist noch Spiegel von Charakter und Persönlichkeit. Veränderungen in ihrem Erscheinungsbild lassen deshalb Rückschlüsse auf den Erregungszustand einer Person zu. Nadine Fecht versteht sich dabei nicht als Schreibende sondern als Zeichnende,

2 Frei zusammengefasst nach: Silvia Matentzoglu, Zur Psychopathologie in den hippokratischen Schriften. Dissertation.de, Erlangen Nürnberg 2011 sowie nach https://de.wiktionary.org/wiki/Hysterie

things, was accompanied by superficial, unstable affectivity and a great need for self-assertion and recognition.[2] By writing "I AM NOT HYSTERICAL", apparently endlessly, Nadine Fecht creates the impression that she has to oppose in writing what has been ingrained in her as a woman, that what she writes in an act of defense is correct, that the opposite claim is false. To this day, when the term "hysteria" is used, it evokes the idea of a female pattern of behavior viewed as pathological, which is interpreted as a lack of self-control, a lack of discipline, resulting in excessive emotion extending to sexual licentiousness.

Repeatedly writing the same sentence using the same word order covering around 240 lines respectively on five largescale sheets of paper is a project which can only be executed by a highly disciplined and self-controlled person. As a consequence, the small arrhythmic displacements of letters and words generated by the handwriting, which lend the rigid framework of sentences a structural shimmer, stand out all the more. Even a controlled handwriting is a reflection of character and personality. As a result, alterations in its appearance provide indications as to a person's state of arousal. Nadine Fecht does not see herself as a writer but as a drawer. Consequently, the lexical content of her script drawings is marginalized while the meaning of their formal appearance is highlighted.

For *hysteria* the artist exclusively uses capital letters in order to lend the script picture the appearance of print, the individual letters that of typeface. Nevertheless, the vertical

2 Freely summarized according to Silvia Matentzoglu, Zur Psychopathologie in den hippokratischen Schriften. Dissertation.de, Erlangen Nuremberg 2011, and after: https://de.wiktionary.org/wiki/Hysterie

structures resulting from the constant sequence of letters in every line display irregularities along the horizontal axis. The script picture is imbued with a disquietude which intensifies towards the center of the five sheets, while gradually abating to the right: A loss of control despite the highly disciplined and disciplining effort of writing? Both yes and no! The excitation, with its seismograph-like traces, is the result of a minimalist conception which plans every variation in advance, and thus, on the contrary, is the expression of the greatest control and discipline. However, the "self-empowerment" which the artist talks about in connection with these drawings is not solely to be found in the mastery of the writing process and its result. The ebbs and flows of the movement and the shimmering disquietude of these script drawings are also a search for form which allows and integrates moods and behavior which up to now have been connoted as female. Consequently *hysteria* can ultimately be understood as an affirmation of a female emotionality and autonomy which has been negatively interpreted by male-dominated psychiatry and, on occasions, devalued to this day.

privileged

In *privileged* Nadine Fecht has written "BEING WHITE BEING WHITE..." without interruption on individual sheets of DIN A4 paper. The right hand edge of the paper determines the line break, irrespective of whether a word or a syllable has been completely written out, so that in many instances the remaining letters are written on the following line.

In formal correspondence to "BEING WHITE BEING..." the artist writes in white ink, and that on black carbon paper. Comparable to a slowly spreading beweb, the white ink appears to occupy new sections of the black surface with every character. Due to the fact that the words are written in capital letters and there is a complete absence of punctuation marks, one can just as easily read "BEING WHITE" as "WHITE BEING", so that in one case the emphasis is placed on the outer appearance, and in the other on an inner essentiality. In addition, as the artist alternates between using two pens with different thicknesses, resulting in varying densities of the color white, lighter and darker areas are formed on the black background. Viewed from a certain distance, these areas are reminiscent of continents on a world map. However, this impression is by no means a chance result. Instead, the artist—as the DIN A4 sheets from which the total area is composed were first written individually—must have followed a largely set choreography with her broader and narrower, compacter and looser lettering, in order to awaken these cartographic associations in the viewer.

However, *privileged* does not just consist of a large format written area with white writing on a black ground. With every letter which is inscribed

wodurch sie den lexikalischen Inhalt marginalisiert und die Bedeutung des formalen Erscheinungsbildes ihrer Schriftzeichnungen unterstreicht.

Für *hysteria* verwendet die Künstlerin ausschließlich Großbuchstaben, um das Schriftbild dem Druck, die einzelnen Buchstaben der Type anzunähern. Dennoch weisen die durch die in jeder Zeile gleichbleibende Buchstabenfolge entstehenden Vertikalstrukturen im horizontalen Verlauf Unregelmäßigkeiten auf. Das Schriftbild durchflimmert eine Unruhe, die sich über die fünf Blätter hinweg zur Mitte hin zusehends steigert, um nach rechts wieder etwas abzuklingen: Kontrollverlust also trotz höchst disziplinierter und disziplinierender Schreibleistung? Ja und nein zugleich! Die wie seismografisch aufgezeichnete Erregung ist das Ergebnis einer minimalistisch jede Variation im Voraus planenden Konzeption und somit gerade umgekehrt Ausdruck allerhöchster Kontrolle und Disziplin. Die „Selbstermächtigung", von der die Künstlerin im Zusammenhang mit diesen Zeichnungen spricht, liegt jedoch nicht allein in der Beherrschung des Schreibvorgangs und dessen Ergebnis. Die zu- und abnehmende Bewegung und die flirrende Unruhe in diesen Schriftzeichnungen sind auch eine bislang weiblich konnotierte Stimmungen und Verhaltensweisen ebenso zulassende wie integrierende Formfindung. Dadurch kann *hysteria* letztlich als die Bejahung einer von männlicher Psychatrie negativ interpretierten, mitunter bis heute abgewerteten weiblichen Emotionalität und Eigenständigkeit verstanden werden.

privileged

Bei *privileged* schreibt Nadine Fecht auf einzelnen DIN-A4-Blättern in jeweils pausenloser Reihung „BEING WHITE BEING WHITE...". Der rechte Blattrand bestimmt den Zeilenumbruch, unabhängig davon, ob ein Wort oder eine Silbe vollständig ausgeschrieben sind, sodass vielfach die zugehörigen Restbuchstaben in der Folgezeile weiterlaufen.

In formaler Entsprechung zu „BEING WHITE BEING..." schreibt die Künstlerin mit weißer Tusche und zwar auf schwarzem Kohlepapier. Einem langsam wuchernden Gespinst vergleichbar, scheint diese weiße Farbe mit jedem Schriftzug neue Partien der schwarzen Fläche zu besetzen. Dadurch, dass die Worte in Versalien geschrieben sind und auf jegliche Satzzeichen verzichtet wird, kann man ebenso „BEING WHITE" lesen wie „WHITE BEING", sodass die Betonung zum einen auf der äußeren Erscheinung und zum anderen auf einer inneren Wesenhaftigkeit liegt. Zudem entstehen, da die Künstlerin phasenweise abwechselnd zwei verschieden dicke Stifte verwendet, aufgrund der unterschiedlichen Dominanz der weißen Farbe hellere und dunklere Bereiche auf dem schwarzen Untergrund. Mit etwas Abstand betrachtet, lassen diese Areale an Kontinente auf einer Weltkarte denken. Dieser Eindruck ist jedoch keineswegs ein zufälliges Ergebnis. Vielmehr muss die Künstlerin – da die DIN-A4-Blätter, aus denen die Gesamtfläche zusammengesetzt ist, zunächst einzeln beschrieben wurden – mit ihren breiteren und schmäleren, dichteren und weiteren Schriftzügen von Anfang an einer weitgehend festgelegten Choreografie gefolgt sein, um schließlich diese kartografischen Assoziationen in den Betrachtenden hervorrufen zu können.

privileged besteht allerdings nicht nur aus einer großformatigen Schreibfläche mit weißer Schrift auf schwarzem Grund. Mit jedem Buchstaben, der dem hauchdünnen Kohlepapier wie einer Haut eingeschrieben wurde, ist zugleich auf einem darunterliegenden großformatigen weißen Blatt in schwarzer Kohle „BEING WHITE BEING…“ durchgepaust worden. Auf diese Weise entsteht ein Diptychon aus den zahlreichen zusammengefügten einzelnen Kohlepapieren mit weißer Schrift auf schwarzem Grund sowie dem Durchdruck in farblicher Umkehrung mit schwarzer Schrift auf weißem Grund. Aufgrund ihrer Entstehung wachsen die beiden Blätter gewissermaßen zu einem Körper zusammen. Wie bei der Verschiebung von „BEING WHITE“ zu „WHITE BEING“ ist auch die farbliche Umkehrung als eine sich gegenseitig bedingende Einheit zu verstehen, die ihre Diptychon-Form absolut zeitgleich ausbildet. Während allerdings auf der schwarzen Pauspapierfläche kontinentale Formationen zu erkennen sind, treten diese auf der weißen Fläche nicht in Erscheinung. Hier ist ausschließlich Text zu lesen, der, als sprichwörtlich „schwarz auf weiß“ gedruckter, in seinem dokumentarischen Charakter wie seiner Aussageintensität nachdrücklich unterstrichen wird.

Lässt man sich auf die assoziative Verweiskraft von *privileged* ein, ist die Verbindung der konzentrierten Aussage „BEING WHITE“ mit der Anmutung einer Weltkarte unschwer als Anspielung auf die Menschheitsgeschichte von Weiß und Schwarz, die Kolonialisierung, Macht und Ohnmacht, Besetzung und Ausbeutung zu verstehen. Ebenso unverkennbar verdeutlicht der Titel, dass die von der schwarzen Fläche unterschiedlich stark besitzergreifenden, weißen Formationen Privilegien genießende Vorherrschaft benennen.

Obgleich die schwarzen Schriftzüge des Durchdrucks ihrer inhaltlichen Aussage „BEING WHITE“ widersprechen, erheben sie als klare, schwarz auf weiß dokumentierte Feststellung Anspruch auf Richtigkeit und fordern Akzeptanz. Weshalb aber der Widerspruch? Bedeutet hier weiß wirklich weiß oder ist weiß nicht vielmehr schwarz? Oder weiß zugleich auch schwarz, schwarz auch weiß? Wenn aber schwarz und weiß nicht eindeutig zu trennen sind, wer ist dann mächtig, wer herrscht und wer ist „privileged“?

Einen Hinweis geben vereinzelt zu entdeckende Flecken, die dort entstanden sind, wo Schreibfehler verbessert oder Wortanfänge korrigiert wurden. Diese kleineren und größeren „Leerstellen“ durchsprenkeln sowohl den weiß auf schwarz geschriebenen Text wie auch dessen schwarz auf weißen Durchdruck – sie markieren Fehler im weißen wie im schwarzen System.

Für den Konzeptkünstler Roman Opalka (1931–2011), der seit Beginn seiner künstlerischen Laufbahn Zahl um Zahl in aufsteigend numerischer Folge aneinandergereiht malte, dokumentiert ein Fehler in seinen Zahlenwerken „die Irreversibilität von Zeit“, denn ein

into the wafer thin, skin-like carbon paper, “BEING WHITE BEING…” is simultaneously traced onto an underlying large-format sheet of white paper in black carbon copy. By this means a diptych is created, composed of the numerous individual sheets of carbon paper with white writing on a black background as well as the color-reversed carbon copy with black writing on a white ground. As a result of their genesis the two sheets fuse, in a manner of speaking, to form one body. As in the case of the shift from “BEING WHITE” to “WHITE BEING”, the color reversal can also be understood as a mutually determined unit, which develops its diptych form in complete simultaneity. However, the continental formations which can be seen on the black carbon paper do not appear on the white surface. Here all that can be seen is text, which literally printed “black on white”, emphatically underlines its documentary character and the intensity of its statement.

If one is receptive to the associative power of *privileged*, then the connection between the concentrated statement “BEING WHITE” and the impression of a world map, then it is not hard to see it as an allusion to the human history of white and black, colonization, power and powerlessness, occupation and exploitation. The title also clearly highlights that the white formations, which take possession of the black surface to varying degrees, represent hegemonies and their privileges.

Although the black letters of the carbon copy contradict their substantive statement “BEING WHITE”, as a clear statement, documented in black and white, they lay claim to truth and demand acceptance. By why the contradiction? Does white really mean white here, or is white not actually black? Or is white simultaneously black, black also white? But if black and white can’t be clearly separated, who is the powerful, who rules, and who is privileged?

A clue is given by individual spots which appear where writing mistakes have been improved or the start of words has been corrected. These “empty spaces” of varying sizes are scattered throughout both the white on black text as well as the black on white carbon copy—they mark errors within both the white and the black system.

For the concept artist Roman Opalka, who since the start of his artistic career has painted number after number in rising numerical sequence, an error in his number works documents “the irreversibility of time”, because an “error emerges quasi as information, and as an example that time really is painted, because one can’t go back, and one can’t undo anything”.[3]

***privileged* from Nadine Fecht also follows time’s linear flow. However, the fields of the individual sheets inscribed in this fashion are less an expression of a purposeful forward motion than an amorphous growth, a slow laminar expansion. In these fields the spots, which seem to emerge without design, appear surprisingly playful, almost like errors in the genetic code of black and white.**

3 Roman Opalka in: Die Irreversibilität von Zeit und die Ewigkeit. Ein Gespräch mit Heinz-Norbert Jocks, Kunstforum vol. 150, April–June 2000, p. 171f.

„Fehler taucht quasi als Information und auch als ein Beispiel dafür auf, dass die Zeit wirklich gemalt ist, weil man nicht zurückgehen und nichts rückgängig machen kann".[3]

Auch *privileged* von Nadine Fecht folgt dem linearen Fluss der Zeit. Die so beschriebenen Felder der einzelnen Blätter verbildlichen dennoch weniger ein zielgerichtetes Vorwärts als ein amorphes Wachsen, ein langsames, flächenhaftes Ausdehnen. In diesen Feldern wirken die wie absichtslos auftauchenden Flecken überraschend spielerisch, fast wie Fehler im genetischen Code von schwarz und weiß.

3 Roman Opalka in: Die Irreversibilität von Zeit und die Ewigkeit. Ein Gespräch mit Heinz-Norbert Jocks, Kunstforum Bd. 150, April–Juni 2000, S. 171f.

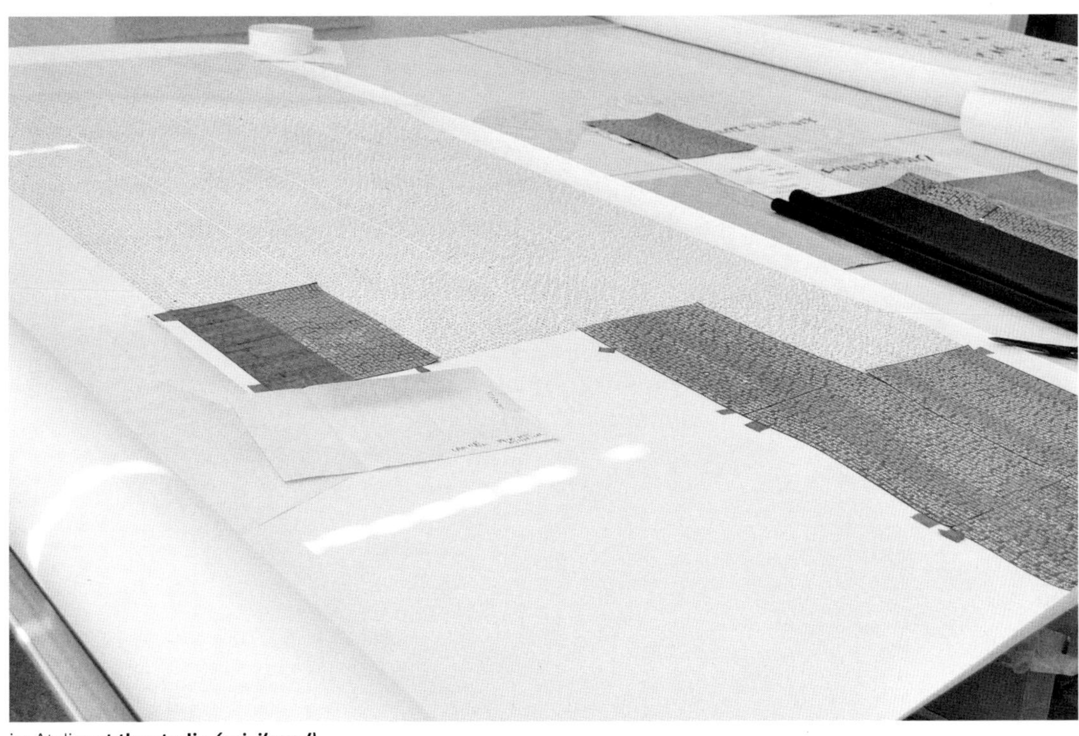

im Atelier **at the studio *(privileged)***

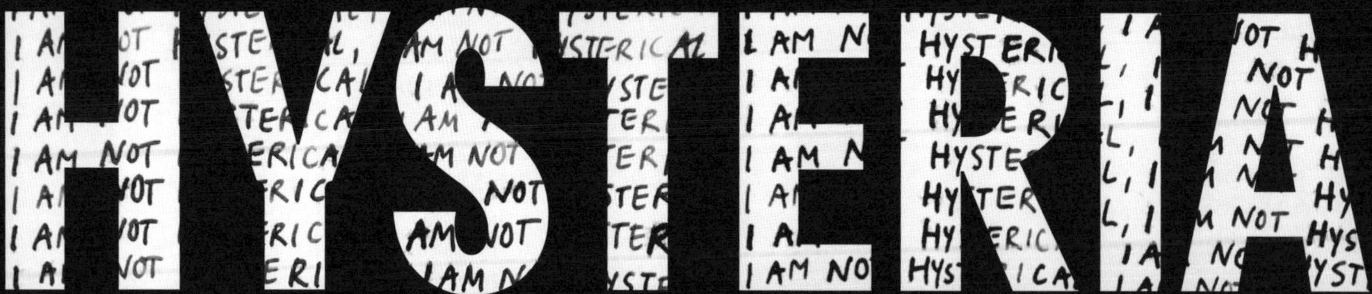
HYSTERIA

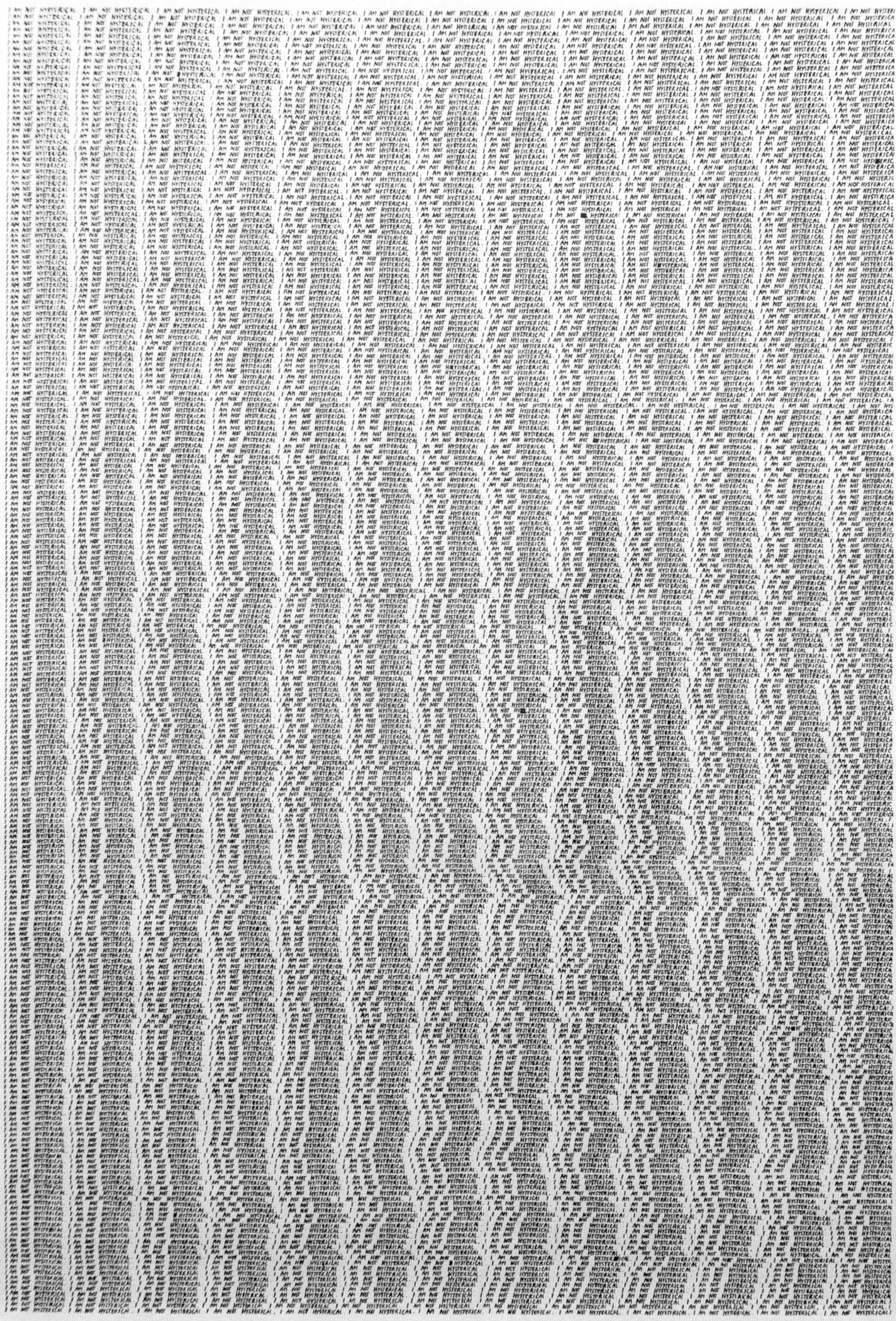
I AM NOT HYSTERICAL

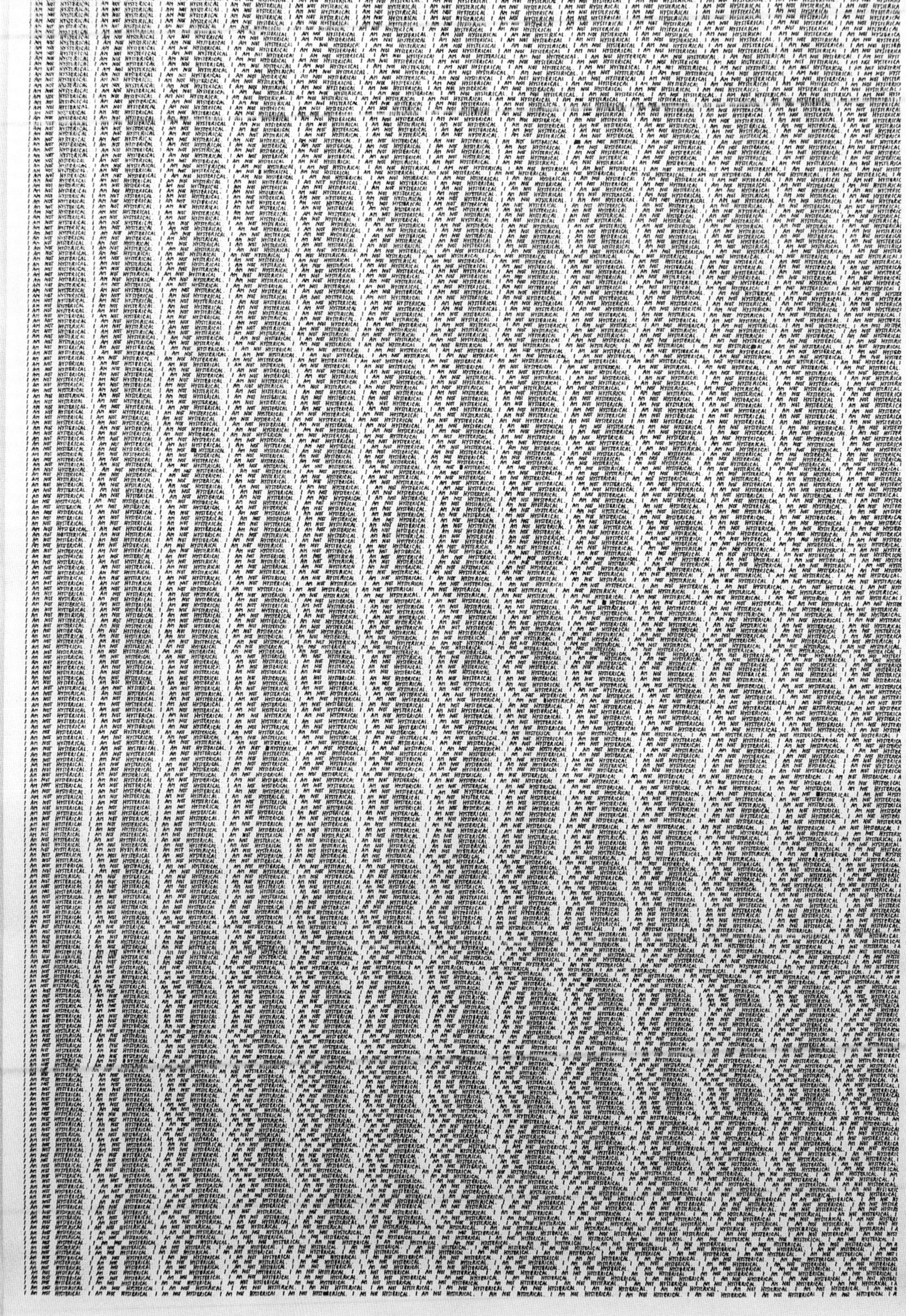
I AM NOT HYSTERICAL

I AM NOT HYSTERICAL I AM NOT HYSTERICAL I AM NOT HYSTERICAL I AM NOT HYSTERICAL I AM NOT HYSTERICAL I AM NOT HYSTERICAL I AM NOT HYSTERICAL I AM NOT HYSTERICAL I AM NOT HYSTERICAL I AM NOT HYSTERICAL I AM NOT HYSTERICAL I AM NOT HYSTERICAL I AM NOT HYSTERICAL I AM NOT HYSTERICAL I AM NOT HYSTE

I AM NOT HYSTERICAL I AM NOT HYSTERICAL I AM NOT HYSTERICAL I AM NOT HYSTERICAL I AM NOT HYSTERICAL I AM NOT HYSTERICAL I AM NOT HYSTERICAL I AM NOT HYSTERICAL I AM NOT HYSTERICAL

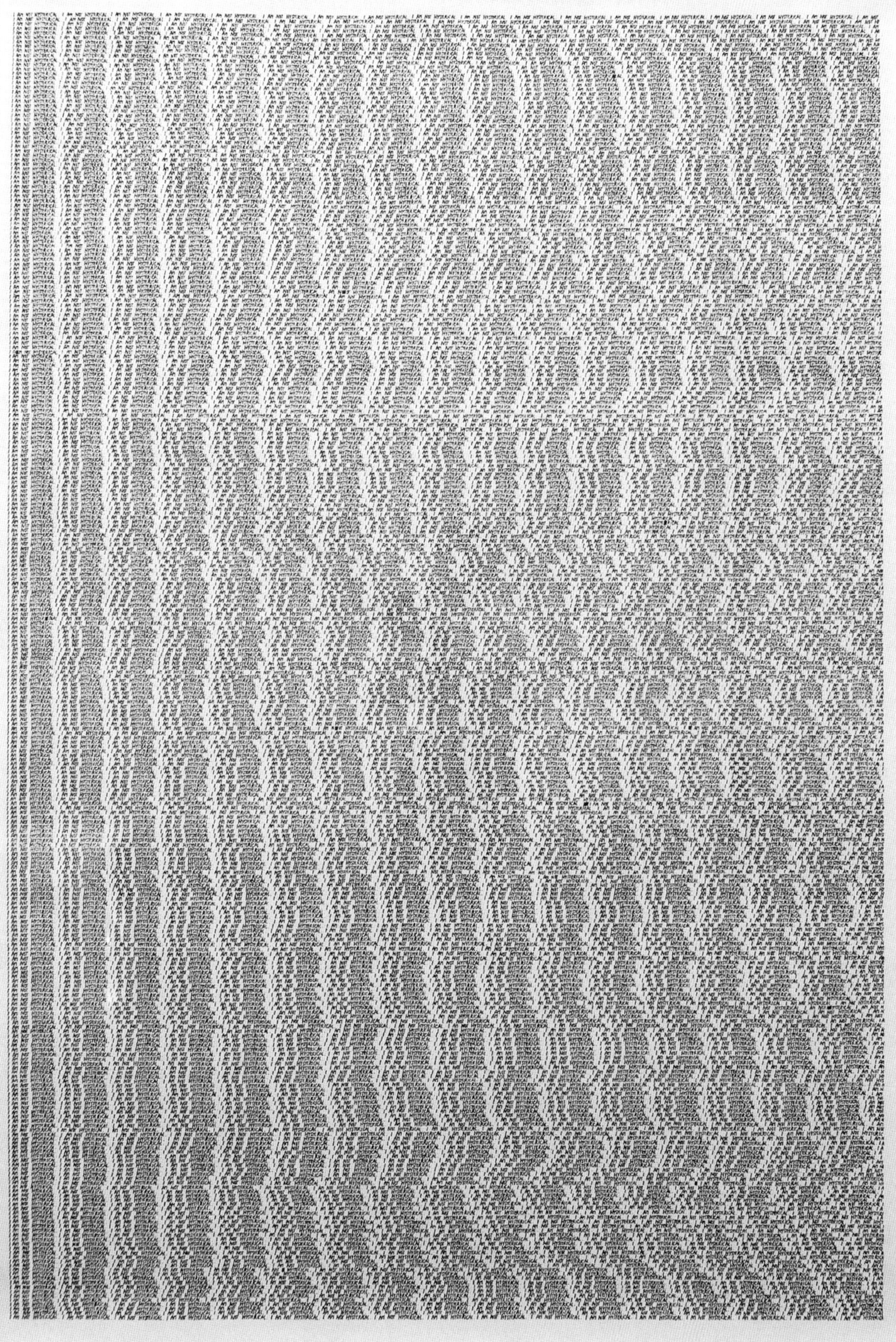

I AM NOT HYSTERICAL. I AM NOT HYSTERICAL. I AM NOT HYSTERICAL. I AM NOT HYSTERICAL. I AM NOT HYSTERICAL. I AM NOT HYSTERICAL.
I AM NOT HYSTERICAL. I AM NOT HYSTERICAL. I AM NOT HYSTERICAL. I AM NOT HYSTERICAL. I AM NOT HYSTERICAL. I AM NOT HYSTERICAL.
I AM NOT HYSTERICAL. I AM NOT HYSTERICAL. I AM NOT HYSTERICAL. I AM NOT HYSTERICAL. I AM NOT HYSTERICAL. I AM NOT HYSTERICAL.
I AM NOT HYSTERICAL. I AM NOT HYSTERICAL. I AM NOT HYSTERICAL. I AM NOT HYSTERICAL. I AM NOT HYSTERICAL. I AM NOT HYSTERICAL.
I AM NOT HYSTERICAL. I AM NOT HYSTERICAL. I AM NOT HYSTERICAL. I AM NOT HYSTERICAL. I AM NOT HYSTERICAL. I AM NOT HYSTERICAL.
I AM NOT HYSTERICAL. I AM NOT HYSTERICAL. I AM NOT HYSTERICAL. I AM NOT HYSTERICAL. I AM NOT HYSTERICAL. I AM NOT HYSTERICAL.
I AM NOT HYSTERICAL. I AM NOT HYSTERICAL. I AM NOT HYSTERICAL. I AM NOT HYSTERICAL. I AM NOT HYSTERICAL. I AM NOT HYSTERICAL.
I AM NOT HYSTERICAL. I AM NOT HYSTERICAL. I AM NOT HYSTERICAL. I AM NOT HYSTERICAL. I AM NOT HYSTERICAL. I AM NOT HYSTERICAL.
I AM NOT HYSTERICAL. I AM NOT HYSTERICAL. I AM NOT HYSTERICAL. I AM NOT HYSTERICAL. I AM NOT HYSTERICAL. I AM NOT HYSTERICAL.
I AM NOT HYSTERICAL. I AM NOT HYSTERICAL. I AM NOT HYSTERICAL. I AM NOT HYSTERICAL. I AM NOT HYSTERICAL. I AM NOT HYSTERICAL.
I AM NOT HYSTERICAL. I AM NOT HYSTERICAL. I AM NOT HYSTERICAL. I AM NOT HYSTERICAL. I AM NOT HYSTERICAL. I AM NOT HYSTERICAL.
I AM NOT HYSTERICAL. I AM NOT HYSTERICAL. I AM NOT HYSTERICAL. I AM NOT HYSTERICAL. I AM NOT HYSTERICAL. I AM NOT HYSTERICAL.
I AM NOT HYSTERICAL. I AM NOT HYSTERICAL. I AM NOT HYSTERICAL. I AM NOT HYSTERICAL. I AM NOT HYSTERICAL. I AM NOT HYSTERICAL.
I AM NOT HYSTERICAL. I AM NOT HYSTERICAL. I AM NOT HYSTERICAL. I AM NOT HYSTERICAL. I AM NOT HYSTERICAL. I AM NOT HYSTERICAL.
I AM NOT HYSTERICAL. I AM NOT HYSTERICAL. I AM NOT HYSTERICAL. I AM NOT HYSTERICAL. I AM NOT HYSTERICAL. I AM NOT HYSTERICAL.
I AM NOT HYSTERICAL. I AM NOT HYSTERICAL. I AM NOT HYSTERICAL. I AM NOT HYSTERICAL. I AM NOT HYSTERICAL. I AM NOT HYSTERICAL.
I AM NOT HYSTERICAL. I AM NOT HYSTERICAL. I AM NOT HYSTERICAL. I AM NOT HYSTERICAL. I AM NOT HYSTERICAL. I AM NOT HYSTERICAL.
I AM NOT HYSTERICAL. I AM NOT HYSTERICAL. I AM NOT HYSTERICAL. I AM NOT HYSTERICAL. I AM NOT HYSTERICAL. I AM NOT HYSTERICAL.
I AM NOT HYSTERICAL. I AM NOT HYSTERICAL. I AM NOT HYSTERICAL. I AM NOT HYSTERICAL. I AM NOT HYSTERICAL. I AM NOT HYSTERICAL.
I AM NOT HYSTERICAL. I AM NOT HYSTERICAL. I AM NOT HYSTERICAL. I AM NOT HYSTERICAL. I AM NOT HYSTERICAL. I AM NOT HYSTERICAL.
I AM NOT HYSTERICAL. I AM NOT HYSTERICAL. I AM NOT HYSTERICAL. I AM NOT HYSTERICAL. I AM NOT HYSTERICAL. I AM NOT HYSTERICAL.
I AM NOT HYSTERICAL. I AM NOT HYSTERICAL. I AM NOT HYSTERICAL. I AM NOT HYSTERICAL. I AM NOT HYSTERICAL. I AM NOT HYSTERICAL.
I AM NOT HYSTERICAL. I AM NOT HYSTERICAL. I AM NOT HYSTERICAL. I AM NOT HYSTERICAL. I AM NOT HYSTERICAL. I AM NOT HYSTERICAL.
I AM NOT HYSTERICAL. I AM NOT HYSTERICAL. I AM NOT HYSTERICAL. I AM NOT HYSTERICAL. I AM NOT HYSTERICAL. I AM NOT HYSTERICAL.
I AM NOT HYSTERICAL. I AM NOT HYSTERICAL. I AM NOT HYSTERICAL. I AM NOT HYSTERICAL. I AM NOT HYSTERICAL. I AM NOT HYSTERICAL.
I AM NOT HYSTERICAL. I AM NOT HYSTERICAL. I AM NOT HYSTERICAL. I AM NOT HYSTERICAL. I AM NOT HYSTERICAL. I AM NOT HYSTERICAL.
I AM NOT HYSTERICAL. I AM NOT HYSTERICAL. I AM NOT HYSTERICAL. I AM NOT HYSTERICAL. I AM NOT HYSTERICAL. I AM NOT HYSTERICAL.
I AM NOT HYSTERICAL. I AM NOT HYSTERICAL. I AM NOT HYSTERICAL. I AM NOT HYSTERICAL. I AM NOT HYSTERICAL. I AM NOT HYSTERICAL.
I AM NOT HYSTERICAL. I AM NOT HYSTERICAL. I AM NOT HYSTERICAL. I AM NOT HYSTERICAL. I AM NOT HYSTERICAL. I AM NOT HYSTERICAL.
I AM NOT HYSTERICAL. I AM NOT HYSTERICAL. I AM NOT HYSTERICAL. I AM NOT HYSTERICAL. I AM NOT HYSTERICAL. I AM NOT HYSTERICAL.
I AM NOT HYSTERICAL. I AM NOT HYSTERICAL. I AM NOT HYSTERICAL. I AM NOT HYSTERICAL. I AM NOT HYSTERICAL. I AM NOT HYSTERICAL.
I AM NOT HYSTERICAL. I AM NOT HYSTERICAL. I AM NOT HYSTERICAL. I AM NOT HYSTERICAL. I AM NOT HYSTERICAL. I AM NOT HYSTERICAL.
I AM NOT HYSTERICAL. I AM NOT HYSTERICAL. I AM NOT HYSTERICAL. I AM NOT HYSTERICAL. I AM NOT HYSTERICAL. I AM NOT HYSTERICAL.
I AM NOT HYSTERICAL. I AM NOT HYSTERICAL. I AM NOT HYSTERICAL. I AM NOT HYSTERICAL. I AM NOT HYSTERICAL. I AM NOT HYSTERICAL.
I AM NOT HYSTERICAL. I AM NOT HYSTERICAL. I AM NOT HYSTERICAL. I AM NOT HYSTERICAL. I AM NOT HYSTERICAL. I AM NOT HYSTERICAL.
I AM NOT HYSTERICAL. I AM NOT HYSTERICAL. I AM NOT HYSTERICAL. I AM NOT HYSTERICAL. I AM NOT HYSTERICAL. I AM NOT HYSTERICAL.
I AM NOT HYSTERICAL. I AM NOT HYSTERICAL. I AM NOT HYSTERICAL. I AM NOT HYSTERICAL. I AM NOT HYSTERICAL. I AM NOT HYSTERICAL.
I AM NOT HYSTERICAL. I AM NOT HYSTERICAL. I AM NOT HYSTERICAL. I AM NOT HYSTERICAL. I AM NOT HYSTERICAL. I AM NOT HYSTERICAL.
I AM NOT HYSTERICAL. I AM NOT HYSTERICAL. I AM NOT HYSTERICAL. I AM NOT HYSTERICAL. I AM NOT HYSTERICAL. I AM NOT HYSTERICAL.
I AM NOT HYSTERICAL. I AM NOT HYSTERICAL. I AM NOT HYSTERICAL. I AM NOT HYSTERICAL. I AM NOT HYSTERICAL. I AM NOT HYSTERICAL.
I AM NOT HYSTERICAL. I AM NOT HYSTERICAL. I AM NOT HYSTERICAL. I AM NOT HYSTERICAL. I AM NOT HYSTERICAL. I AM NOT HYSTERICAL.
I AM NOT HYSTERICAL. I AM NOT HYSTERICAL. I AM NOT HYSTERICAL. I AM NOT HYSTERICAL. I AM NOT HYSTERICAL. I AM NOT HYSTERICAL.
I AM NOT HYSTERICAL. I AM NOT HYSTERICAL. I AM NOT HYSTERICAL. I AM NOT HYSTERICAL. I AM NOT HYSTERICAL. I AM NOT HYSTERICAL.
I AM NOT HYSTERICAL. I AM NOT HYSTERICAL. I AM NOT HYSTERICAL. I AM NOT HYSTERICAL. I AM NOT HYSTERICAL. I AM NOT HYSTERICAL.
I AM NOT HYSTERICAL. I AM NOT HYSTERICAL. I AM NOT HYSTERICAL. I AM NOT HYSTERICAL. I AM NOT HYSTERICAL. I AM NOT HYSTERICAL.
I AM NOT HYSTERICAL. I AM NOT HYSTERICAL. I AM NOT HYSTERICAL. I AM NOT HYSTERICAL. I AM NOT HYSTERICAL. I AM NOT HYSTERICAL.
I AM NOT HYSTERICAL. I AM NOT HYSTERICAL. I AM NOT HYSTERICAL. I AM NOT HYSTERICAL. I AM NOT HYSTERICAL. I AM NOT HYSTERICAL.
I AM NOT HYSTERICAL. I AM NOT HYSTERICAL. I AM NOT HYSTERICAL. I AM NOT HYSTERICAL. I AM NOT HYSTERICAL. I AM NOT HYSTERICAL.
I AM NOT HYSTERICAL. I AM NOT HYSTERICAL. I AM NOT HYSTERICAL. I AM NOT HYSTERICAL. I AM NOT HYSTERICAL. I AM NOT HYSTERICAL.
I AM NOT HYSTERICAL. I AM NOT HYSTERICAL. I AM NOT HYSTERICAL. I AM NOT HYSTERICAL. I AM NOT HYSTERICAL. I AM NOT HYSTERICAL.
I AM NOT HYSTERICAL. I AM NOT HYSTERICAL. I AM NOT HYSTERICAL. I AM NOT HYSTERICAL. I AM NOT HYSTERICAL. I AM NOT HYSTERICAL.
I AM NOT HYSTERICAL. I AM NOT HYSTERICAL. I AM NOT HYSTERICAL. I AM NOT HYSTERICAL. I AM NOT HYSTERICAL. I AM NOT HYSTERICAL.
I AM NOT HYSTERICAL. I AM NOT HYSTERICAL. I AM NOT HYSTERICAL. I AM NOT HYSTERICAL. I AM NOT HYSTERICAL. I AM NOT HYSTERICAL.
I AM NOT HYSTERICAL. I AM NOT HYSTERICAL. I AM NOT HYSTERICAL. I AM NOT HYSTERICAL. I AM NOT HYSTERICAL. I AM NOT HYSTERICAL.
I AM NOT HYSTERICAL. I AM NOT HYSTERICAL. I AM NOT HYSTERICAL. I AM NOT HYSTERICAL. I AM NOT HYSTERICAL. I AM NOT HYSTERICAL.
I AM NOT HYSTERICAL. I AM NOT HYSTERICAL. I AM NOT HYSTERICAL. I AM NOT HYSTERICAL. I AM NOT HYSTERICAL. I AM NOT HYSTERICAL.
I AM NOT HYSTERICAL. I AM NOT HYSTERICAL. I AM NOT HYSTERICAL. I AM NOT HYSTERICAL. I AM NOT HYSTERICAL. I AM NOT HYSTERICAL.
I AM NOT HYSTERICAL. I AM NOT HYSTERICAL. I AM NOT HYSTERICAL. I AM NOT HYSTERICAL. I AM NOT HYSTERICAL. I AM NOT HYSTERICAL.
I AM NOT HYSTERICAL. I AM NOT HYSTERICAL. I AM NOT HYSTERICAL. I AM NOT HYSTERICAL. I AM NOT HYSTERICAL. I AM NOT HYSTERICAL.
I AM NOT HYSTERICAL. I AM NOT HYSTERICAL. I AM NOT HYSTERICAL. I AM NOT HYSTERICAL. I AM NOT HYSTERICAL. I AM NOT HYSTERICAL.
I AM NOT HYSTERICAL. I AM NOT HYSTERICAL. I AM NOT HYSTERICAL. I AM NOT HYSTERICAL. I AM NOT HYSTERICAL. I AM NOT HYSTERICAL.
I AM NOT HYSTERICAL. I AM NOT HYSTERICAL. I AM NOT HYSTERICAL. I AM NOT HYSTERICAL. I AM NOT HYSTERICAL. I AM NOT HYSTERICAL.
I AM NOT HYSTERICAL. I AM NOT HYSTERICAL. I AM NOT HYSTERICAL. I AM NOT HYSTERICAL. I AM NOT HYSTERICAL. I AM NOT HYSTERICAL.
I AM NOT HYSTERICAL. I AM NOT HYSTERICAL. I AM NOT HYSTERICAL. I AM NOT HYSTERICAL. I AM NOT HYSTERICAL. I AM NOT HYSTERICAL.
I AM NOT HYSTERICAL. I AM NOT HYSTERICAL. I AM NOT HYSTERICAL. I AM NOT HYSTERICAL. I AM NOT HYSTERICAL. I AM NOT HYSTERICAL.
I AM NOT HYSTERICAL. I AM NOT HYSTERICAL. I AM NOT HYSTERICAL. I AM NOT HYSTERICAL. I AM NOT HYSTERICAL. I AM NOT HYSTERICAL.
I AM NOT HYSTERICAL. I AM NOT HYSTERICAL. I AM NOT HYSTERICAL. I AM NOT HYSTERICAL. I AM NOT HYSTERICAL. I AM NOT HYSTERICAL.
I AM NOT HYSTERICAL. I AM NOT HYSTERICAL. I AM NOT HYSTERICAL. I AM NOT HYSTERICAL. I AM NOT HYSTERICAL. I AM NOT HYSTERICAL.
I AM NOT HYSTERICAL. I AM NOT HYSTERICAL. I AM NOT HYSTERICAL. I AM NOT HYSTERICAL. I AM NOT HYSTERICAL. I AM NOT HYSTERICAL.
I AM NOT HYSTERICAL. I AM NOT HYSTERICAL. I AM NOT HYSTERICAL. I AM NOT HYSTERICAL. I AM NOT HYSTERICAL. I AM NOT HYSTERICAL.
I AM NOT HYSTERICAL. I AM NOT HYSTERICAL. I AM NOT HYSTERICAL. I AM NOT HYSTERICAL. I AM NOT HYSTERICAL. I AM NOT HYSTERICAL.
I AM NOT HYSTERICAL. I AM NOT HYSTERICAL. I AM NOT HYSTERICAL. I AM NOT HYSTERICAL. I AM NOT HYSTERICAL. I AM NOT HYSTERICAL.
I AM NOT HYSTERICAL. I AM NOT HYSTERICAL. I AM NOT HYSTERICAL. I AM NOT HYSTERICAL. I AM NOT HYSTERICAL. I AM NOT HYSTERICAL.
I AM NOT HYSTERICAL. I AM NOT HYSTERICAL. I AM NOT HYSTERICAL. I AM NOT HYSTERICAL. I AM NOT HYSTERICAL. I AM NOT HYSTERICAL.
I AM NOT HYSTERICAL. I AM NOT HYSTERICAL. I AM NOT HYSTERICAL. I AM NOT HYSTERICAL. I AM NOT HYSTERICAL. I AM NOT HYSTERICAL.
I AM NOT HYSTERICAL. I AM NOT HYSTERICAL. I AM NOT HYSTERICAL. I AM NOT HYSTERICAL. I AM NOT HYSTERICAL. I AM NOT HYSTERICAL.
I AM NOT HYSTERICAL. I AM NOT HYSTERICAL. I AM NOT HYSTERICAL. I AM NOT HYSTERICAL. I AM NOT HYSTERICAL. I AM NOT HYSTERICAL.
I AM NOT HYSTERICAL. I AM NOT HYSTERICAL. I AM NOT HYSTERICAL. I AM NOT HYSTERICAL. I AM NOT HYSTERICAL. I AM NOT HYSTERICAL.
I AM NOT HYSTERICAL. I AM NOT HYSTERICAL. I AM NOT HYSTERICAL. I AM NOT HYSTERICAL. I AM NOT HYSTERICAL. I AM NOT HYSTERICAL.
I AM NOT HYSTERICAL. I AM NOT HYSTERICAL. I AM NOT HYSTERICAL. I AM NOT HYSTERICAL. I AM NOT HYSTERICAL. I AM NOT HYSTERICAL.
I AM NOT HYSTERICAL. I AM NOT HYSTERICAL. I AM NOT HYSTERICAL. I AM NOT HYSTERICAL. I AM NOT HYSTERICAL. I AM NOT HYSTERICAL.
I AM NOT HYSTERICAL. I AM NOT HYSTERICAL. I AM NOT HYSTERICAL. I AM NOT HYSTERICAL. I AM NOT HYSTERICAL. I AM NOT HYSTERICAL.
I AM NOT HYSTERICAL. I AM NOT HYSTERICAL. I AM NOT HYSTERICAL. I AM NOT HYSTERICAL. I AM NOT HYSTERICAL. I AM NOT HYSTERICAL.
I AM NOT HYSTERICAL. I AM NOT HYSTERICAL. I AM NOT HYSTERICAL. I AM NOT HYSTERICAL. I AM NOT HYSTERICAL. I AM NOT HYSTERICAL.
I AM NOT HYSTERICAL. I AM NOT HYSTERICAL. I AM NOT HYSTERICAL. I AM NOT HYSTERICAL. I AM NOT HYSTERICAL. I AM NOT HYSTERICAL.
I AM NOT HYSTERICAL. I AM NOT HYSTERICAL. I AM NOT HYSTERICAL. I AM NOT HYSTERICAL. I AM NOT HYSTERICAL. I AM NOT HYSTERICAL.
I AM NOT HYSTERICAL. I AM NOT HYSTERICAL. I AM NOT HYSTERICAL. I AM NOT HYSTERICAL. I AM NOT HYSTERICAL. I AM NOT HYSTERICAL.
I AM NOT HYSTERICAL. I AM NOT HYSTERICAL. I AM NOT HYSTERICAL. I AM NOT HYSTERICAL. I AM NOT HYSTERICAL. I AM NOT HYSTERICAL.
I AM NOT HYSTERICAL. I AM NOT HYSTERICAL. I AM NOT HYSTERICAL. I AM NOT HYSTERICAL. I AM NOT HYSTERICAL. I AM NOT HYSTERICAL.
I AM NOT HYSTERICAL. I AM NOT HYSTERICAL. I AM NOT HYSTERICAL. I AM NOT HYSTERICAL. I AM NOT HYSTERICAL. I AM NOT HYSTERICAL.
I AM NOT HYSTERICAL. I AM NOT HYSTERICAL. I AM NOT HYSTERICAL. I AM NOT HYSTERICAL. I AM NOT HYSTERICAL. I AM NOT HYSTERICAL.
I AM NOT HYSTERICAL. I AM NOT HYSTERICAL. I AM NOT HYSTERICAL. I AM NOT HYSTERICAL. I AM NOT HYSTERICAL. I AM NOT HYSTERICAL.
I AM NOT HYSTERICAL. I AM NOT HYSTERICAL. I AM NOT HYSTERICAL. I AM NOT HYSTERICAL. I AM NOT HYSTERICAL. I AM NOT HYSTERICAL.
I AM NOT HYSTERICAL. I AM NOT HYSTERICAL. I AM NOT HYSTERICAL. I AM NOT HYSTERICAL. I AM NOT HYSTERICAL. I AM NOT HYSTERICAL.
I AM NOT HYSTERICAL. I AM NOT HYSTERICAL. I AM NOT HYSTERICAL. I AM NOT HYSTERICAL. I AM NOT HYSTERICAL. I AM NOT HYSTERICAL.
I AM NOT HYSTERICAL. I AM NOT HYSTERICAL. I AM NOT HYSTERICAL. I AM NOT HYSTERICAL. I AM NOT HYSTERICAL. I AM NOT HYSTERICAL.
I AM NOT HYSTERICAL. I AM NOT HYSTERICAL. I AM NOT HYSTERICAL. I AM NOT HYSTERICAL. I AM NOT HYSTERICAL. I AM NOT HYSTERICAL.
I AM NOT HYSTERICAL. I AM NOT HYSTERICAL. I AM NOT HYSTERICAL. I AM NOT HYSTERICAL. I AM NOT HYSTERICAL. I AM NOT HYSTERICAL.
I AM NOT HYSTERICAL. I AM NOT HYSTERICAL. I AM NOT HYSTERICAL. I AM NOT HYSTERICAL. I AM NOT HYSTERICAL. I AM NOT HYSTERICAL.
I AM NOT HYSTERICAL. I AM NOT HYSTERICAL. I AM NOT HYSTERICAL. I AM NOT HYSTERICAL. I AM NOT HYSTERICAL. I AM NOT HYSTERICAL.
I AM NOT HYSTERICAL. I AM NOT HYSTERICAL. I AM NOT HYSTERICAL. I AM NOT HYSTERICAL. I AM NOT HYSTERICAL. I AM NOT HYSTERICAL.
I AM NOT HYSTERICAL. I AM NOT HYSTERICAL. I AM NOT HYSTERICAL. I AM NOT HYSTERICAL. I AM NOT HYSTERICAL. I AM NOT HYSTERICAL.
I AM NOT HYSTERICAL. I AM NOT HYSTERICAL. I AM NOT HYSTERICAL. I AM NOT HYSTERICAL. I AM NOT HYSTERICAL. I AM NOT HYSTERICAL.
I AM NOT HYSTERICAL. I AM NOT HYSTERICAL. I AM NOT HYSTERICAL. I AM NOT HYSTERICAL. I AM NOT HYSTERICAL. I AM NOT HYSTERICAL.
I AM NOT HYSTERICAL. I AM NOT HYSTERICAL. I AM NOT HYSTERICAL. I AM NOT HYSTERICAL. I AM NOT HYSTERICAL. I AM NOT HYSTERICAL.
I AM NOT HYSTERICAL. I AM NOT HYSTERICAL. I AM NOT HYSTERICAL. I AM NOT HYSTERICAL. I AM NOT HYSTERICAL. I AM NOT HYSTERICAL.
I AM NOT HYSTERICAL. I AM NOT HYSTERICAL. I AM NOT HYSTERICAL. I AM NOT HYSTERICAL. I AM NOT HYSTERICAL. I AM NOT HYSTERICAL.
I AM NOT HYSTERICAL. I AM NOT HYSTERICAL. I AM NOT HYSTERICAL. I AM NOT HYSTERICAL. I AM NOT HYSTERICAL. I AM NOT HYSTERICAL.
I AM NOT HYSTERICAL. I AM NOT HYSTERICAL. I AM NOT HYSTERICAL. I AM NOT HYSTERICAL. I AM NOT HYSTERICAL. I AM NOT HYSTERICAL.
I AM NOT HYSTERICAL. I AM NOT HYSTERICAL. I AM NOT HYSTERICAL. I AM NOT HYSTERICAL. I AM NOT HYSTERICAL. I AM NOT HYSTERICAL.

RICAL. I AM NOT HYSTERICAL. I AM NOT HYSTERICAL. I AM NOT HYSTERICAL. I AM NOT HYSTERICAL. I AM NOT HYSTERICAL. I AM HYS
STERICAL. I AM NOT HYSTERICAL. I AM NOT HYSTERICAL. I AM NOT HYSTERICAL. I AM NOT HYSTERICAL. I AM NOT HYSTERICAL. I AM NOT HYS
RICAL. I AM NOT HYSTERICAL. I AM NOT HYSTERICAL. I AM NOT HYSTERICAL. I AM NOT HYSTERICAL. I AM NOT HYSTERICAL. I AM NOT HYSTERI
ICAL. I AM NOT HYSTERICAL. I AM NOT HYSTERICAL. I AM NOT HYSTERICAL. I AM NOT HYSTERICAL. I AM NOT HYSTERICAL. I AM NOT HYSTERI
RICAL. I AM NOT HYSTERICAL. I AM NOT HYSTERICAL. I AM NOT HYSTERICAL. I AM NOT HYSTERICAL. I AM NOT HYSTERICAL. I AM NOT HYSTE
CAL. I AM NOT HYSTERICAL. I AM NOT HYSTERICAL. I AM NOT HYSTERICAL. I AM NOT HYSTERICAL. I AM NOT HYSTERICAL. I AM NOT HYSTERIC
TERICAL. I AM NOT HYSTERICAL. I AM NOT HYSTERICAL. I AM NOT HYSTERICAL. I AM NOT HYSTERICAL. I AM NOT HYSTERICAL. I AM NOT HYST
HYSTERICAL. I AM NOT HYSTERICAL. I AM NOT HYSTERICAL. I AM NOT HYSTERICAL. I AM NOT HYSTERICAL. I AM NOT HYSTERICAL. I AM NOT HYS
CAL. I AM NOT HYSTERICAL. I AM NOT HYSTERICAL. I AM NOT HYSTERICAL. I AM NOT HYSTERICAL. I AM NOT HYSTERICAL. I AM NOT HYSTERICAL
CAL. I AM NOT HYSTERICAL. I AM NOT HYSTERICAL. I AM NOT HYSTERICAL. I AM NOT HYSTERICAL. I AM NOT HYSTERICAL. I AM NOT HYSTERICA
ERICAL. I AM NOT HYSTERICAL. I AM NOT HYSTERICAL. I AM NOT HYSTERICAL. I AM NOT HYSTERICAL. I AM NOT HYSTERICAL. I AM NOT HYSTERIC
TERICAL. I AM NOT HYSTERICAL. I AM NOT HYSTERICAL. I AM NOT HYSTERICAL. I AM NOT HYSTERICAL. I AM NOT HYSTERICAL. I AM NOT HYSTER
RICAL. I AM NOT HYSTERICAL. I AM NOT HYSTERICAL. I AM NOT HYSTERICAL. I AM NOT HYSTERICAL. I AM NOT HYSTERICAL. I AM NOT HYSTE
CAL. I AM NOT HYSTERICAL. I AM NOT HYSTERICAL. I AM NOT HYSTERICAL. I AM NOT HYSTERICAL. I AM NOT HYSTERICAL. I AM NOT HYSTERIC
RICAL. I AM NOT HYSTERICAL. I AM NOT HYSTERICAL. I AM NOT HYSTERICAL. I AM NOT HYSTERICAL. I AM NOT HYSTERICAL. I AM NOT HYSTER
RICAL. I AM NOT HYSTERICAL. I AM NOT HYSTERICAL. I AM NOT HYSTERICAL. I AM NOT HYSTERICAL. I AM NOT HYSTERICAL. I AM NOT HYSTERI
RICAL. I AM NOT HYSTERICAL. I AM NOT HYSTERICAL. I AM NOT HYSTERICAL. I AM NOT HYSTERICAL. I AM NOT HYSTERICAL. I AM NOT HYSTER
ERICAL. I AM NOT HYSTERICAL. I AM NOT HYSTERICAL. I AM NOT HYSTERICAL. I AM NOT HYSTERICAL. I AM NOT HYSTERICAL. I AM NOT HYSTER
RICAL. I AM NOT HYSTERICAL. I AM NOT HYSTERICAL. I AM NOT HYSTERICAL. I AM NOT HYSTERICAL. I AM NOT HYSTERICAL. I AM NOT HYSTER
CAL. I AM NOT HYSTERICAL. I AM NOT HYSTERICAL. I AM NOT HYSTERICAL. I AM NOT HYSTERICAL. I AM NOT HYSTERICAL. I AM NOT HYSTER
ERICAL. I AM NOT HYSTERICAL. I AM NOT HYSTERICAL. I AM NOT HYSTERICAL. I AM NOT HYSTERICAL. I AM NOT HYSTERICAL. I AM NOT HYST
TERICAL. I AM NOT HYSTERICAL. I AM NOT HYSTERICAL. I AM NOT HYSTERICAL. I AM NOT HYSTERICAL. I AM NOT HYSTERICAL. I AM NOT HYS
ICAL. I AM NOT HYSTERICAL. I AM NOT HYSTERICAL. I AM NOT HYSTERICAL. I AM NOT HYSTERICAL. I AM NOT HYSTERICAL. I AM NOT HYSTER
ERICAL. I AM NOT HYSTERICAL. I AM NOT HYSTERICAL. I AM NOT HYSTERICAL. I AM NOT HYSTERICAL. I AM NOT HYSTERICAL. I AM NOT HYSTER
ERICAL. I AM NOT HYSTERICAL. I AM NOT HYSTERICAL. I AM NOT HYSTERICAL. I AM NOT HYSTERICAL. I AM NOT HYSTERICAL. I AM NOT HYSTE
RICAL. I AM NOT HYSTERICAL. I AM NOT HYSTERICAL. I AM NOT HYSTERICAL. I AM NOT HYSTERICAL. I AM NOT HYSTERICAL. I AM NOT HYSTER
ICAL. I AM NOT HYSTERICAL. I AM NOT HYSTERICAL. I AM NOT HYSTERICAL. I AM NOT HYSTERICAL. I AM NOT HYSTERICAL. I AM NOT HYSTERI
ICAL. I AM NOT HYSTERICAL. I AM NOT HYSTERICAL. I AM NOT HYSTERICAL. I AM NOT HYSTERICAL. I AM NOT HYSTERICAL. I AM NOT HYSTERICA
ERICAL. I AM NOT HYSTERICAL. I AM NOT HYSTERICAL. I AM NOT HYSTERICAL. I AM NOT HYSTERICAL. I AM NOT HYSTERICAL. I AM NOT HYSTERIC
ERICAL. I AM NOT HYSTERICAL. I AM NOT HYSTERICAL. I AM NOT HYSTERICAL. I AM NOT HYSTERICAL. I AM NOT HYSTERICAL. I AM NOT HYSTE
ICAL. I AM NOT HYSTERICAL. I AM NOT HYSTERICAL. I AM NOT HYSTERICAL. I AM NOT HYSTERICAL. I AM NOT HYSTERICAL. I AM NOT HYSTER
TERICAL. I AM NOT HYSTERICAL. I AM NOT HYSTERICAL. I AM NOT HYSTERICAL. I AM NOT HYSTERICAL. I AM NOT HYSTERICAL. I AM NOT HYSTE
STERICAL. I AM NOT HYSTERICAL. I AM NOT HYSTERICAL. I AM NOT HYSTERICAL. I AM NOT HYSTERICAL. I AM NOT HYSTERICAL. I AM NOT HYS
ERICAL. I AM NOT HYSTERICAL. I AM NOT HYSTERICAL. I AM NOT HYSTERICAL. I AM NOT HYSTERICAL. I AM NOT HYSTERICAL. I AM NOT HYSTERICA
STERICAL. I AM NOT HYSTERICAL. I AM NOT HYSTERICAL. I AM NOT HYSTERICAL. I AM NOT HYSTERICAL. I AM NOT HYSTERICAL. I AM NOT HYS
TERICAL. I AM NOT HYSTERICAL. I AM NOT HYSTERICAL. I AM NOT HYSTERICAL. I AM NOT HYSTERICAL. I AM NOT HYSTERICAL. I AM NOT HYS
STERICAL. I AM NOT HYSTERICAL. I AM NOT HYSTERICAL. I AM NOT HYSTERICAL. I AM NOT HYSTERICAL. I AM NOT HYSTERICAL. I AM NOT HYS
ERICAL. I AM NOT HYSTERICAL. I AM NOT HYSTERICAL. I AM NOT HYSTERICAL. I AM NOT HYSTERICAL. I AM NOT HYSTERICAL. I AM NOT HYSTERI
STERICAL. I AM NOT HYSTERICAL. I AM NOT HYSTERICAL. I AM NOT HYSTERICAL. I AM NOT HYSTERICAL. I AM NOT HYSTERICAL. I AM NOT HYSTE
STERICAL. I AM NOT HYSTERICAL. I AM NOT HYSTERICAL. I AM NOT HYSTERICAL. I AM NOT HYSTERICAL. I AM NOT HYSTERICAL. I AM NOT HYS
TERICAL. I AM NOT HYSTERICAL. I AM NOT HYSTERICAL. I AM NOT HYSTERICAL. I AM NOT HYSTERICAL. I AM NOT HYSTERICAL. I AM NOT HYSTER
TERICAL. I AM NOT HYSTERICAL. I AM NOT HYSTERICAL. I AM NOT HYSTERICAL. I AM NOT HYSTERICAL. I AM NOT HYSTERICAL. I AM NOT HYST
TERICAL. I AM NOT HYSTERICAL. I AM NOT HYSTERICAL. I AM NOT HYSTERICAL. I AM NOT HYSTERICAL. I AM NOT HYSTERICAL. I AM NOT HYSTERIC
RICAL. I AM NOT HYSTERICAL. I AM NOT HYSTERICAL. I AM NOT HYSTERICAL. I AM NOT HYSTERICAL. I AM NOT HYSTERICAL. I AM NOT HYS
ERICAL. I AM NOT HYSTERICAL. I AM NOT HYSTERICAL. I AM NOT HYSTERICAL. I AM NOT HYSTERICAL. I AM NOT HYSTERICAL. I AM NOT HYSTER
STERICAL. I AM NOT HYSTERICAL. I AM NOT HYSTERICAL. I AM NOT HYSTERICAL. I AM NOT HYSTERICAL. I AM NOT HYSTERICAL. I AM NOT HYS
TERICAL. I AM NOT HYSTERICAL. I AM NOT HYSTERICAL. I AM NOT HYSTERICAL. I AM NOT HYSTERICAL. I AM NOT HYSTERICAL. I AM NOT H
RICAL. I AM NOT HYSTERICAL. I AM NOT HYSTERICAL. I AM NOT HYSTERICAL. I AM NOT HYSTERICAL. I AM NOT HYSTERICAL. I AM NOT HYS
RICAL. I AM NOT HYSTERICAL. I AM NOT HYSTERICAL. I AM NOT HYSTERICAL. I AM NOT HYSTERICAL. I AM NOT HYSTERICAL. I AM NOT HYSTERIC
RICAL. I AM NOT HYSTERICAL. I AM NOT HYSTERICAL. I AM NOT HYSTERICAL. I AM NOT HYSTERICAL. I AM NOT HYSTERICAL. I AM NOT HYSTERI
ERICAL. I AM NOT HYSTERICAL. I AM NOT HYSTERICAL. I AM NOT HYSTERICAL. I AM NOT HYSTERICAL. I AM NOT HYSTERICAL. I AM NOT H
CAL. I AM NOT HYSTERICAL. I AM NOT HYSTERICAL. I AM NOT HYSTERICAL. I AM NOT HYSTERICAL. I AM NOT HYSTERICAL. I AM NOT HYSTERIC
RICAL. I AM NOT HYSTERICAL. I AM NOT HYSTERICAL. I AM NOT HYSTERICAL. I AM NOT HYSTERICAL. I AM NOT HYSTERICAL. I AM NOT HYSTERIC
ERICAL. I AM NOT HYSTERICAL. I AM NOT HYSTERICAL. I AM NOT HYSTERICAL. I AM NOT HYSTERICAL. I AM NOT HYSTERICAL. I AM NOT HY
TERICAL. I AM NOT HYSTERICAL. I AM NOT HYSTERICAL. I AM NOT HYSTERICAL. I AM NOT HYSTERICAL. I AM NOT HYSTERICAL. I AM NOT HYSTERIC
TERICAL. I AM NOT HYSTERICAL. I AM NOT HYSTERICAL. I AM NOT HYSTERICAL. I AM NOT HYSTERICAL. I AM NOT HYSTERICAL. I AM NOT HYSTERIC
STERICAL. I AM NOT HYSTERICAL. I AM NOT HYSTERICAL. I AM NOT HYSTERICAL. I AM NOT HYSTERICAL. I AM NOT HYSTERICAL. I AM NOT HYSTE
STERICAL. I AM NOT HYSTERICAL. I AM NOT HYSTERICAL. I AM NOT HYSTERICAL. I AM NOT HYSTERICAL. I AM NOT HYSTERICAL. I AM NOT HYSTER
STERICAL. I AM NOT HYSTERICAL. I AM NOT HYSTERICAL. I AM NOT HYSTERICAL. I AM NOT HYSTERICAL. I AM NOT HYSTERICAL. I AM NOT HYSTER
RICAL. I AM NOT HYSTERICAL. I AM NOT HYSTERICAL. I AM NOT HYSTERICAL. I AM NOT HYSTERICAL. I AM NOT HYSTERICAL. I AM NOT HYSTER
ICAL. I AM NOT HYSTERICAL. I AM NOT HYSTERICAL. I AM NOT HYSTERICAL. I AM NOT HYSTERICAL. I AM NOT HYSTERICAL. I AM NOT HYSTERICAL
STERICAL. I AM NOT HYSTERICAL. I AM NOT HYSTERICAL. I AM NOT HYSTERICAL. I AM NOT HYSTERICAL. I AM NOT HYSTERICAL. I AM NOT HYSTERIC
CAL. I AM NOT HYSTERICAL. I AM NOT HYSTERICAL. I AM NOT HYSTERICAL. I AM NOT HYSTERICAL. I AM NOT HYSTERICAL. I AM NOT HYSTERICA
RICAL. I AM NOT HYSTERICAL. I AM NOT HYSTERICAL. I AM NOT HYSTERICAL. I AM NOT HYSTERICAL. I AM NOT HYSTERICAL. I AM NOT HYS
TERICAL. I AM NOT HYSTERICAL. I AM NOT HYSTERICAL. I AM NOT HYSTERICAL. I AM NOT HYSTERICAL. I AM NOT HYSTERICAL. I AM NOT HY
RICAL. I AM NOT HYSTERICAL. I AM NOT HYSTERICAL. I AM NOT HYSTERICAL. I AM NOT HYSTERICAL. I AM NOT HYSTERICAL. I AM NOT HYSTE
RICAL. I AM NOT HYSTERICAL. I AM NOT HYSTERICAL. I AM NOT HYSTERICAL. I AM NOT HYSTERICAL. I AM NOT HYSTERICAL. I AM NOT HYSTER
ERICAL. I AM NOT HYSTERICAL. I AM NOT HYSTERICAL. I AM NOT HYSTERICAL. I AM NOT HYSTERICAL. I AM NOT HYSTERICAL. I AM NOT HYSTERI
ERICAL. I AM NOT HYSTERICAL. I AM NOT HYSTERICAL. I AM NOT HYSTERICAL. I AM NOT HYSTERICAL. I AM NOT HYSTERICAL. I AM NOT HYSTER
ERICAL. I AM NOT HYSTERICAL. I AM NOT HYSTERICAL. I AM NOT HYSTERICAL. I AM NOT HYSTERICAL. I AM NOT HYSTERICAL. I AM NOT HYSTER
STERICAL. I AM NOT HYSTERICAL. I AM NOT HYSTERICAL. I AM NOT HYSTERICAL. I AM NOT HYSTERICAL. I AM NOT HYSTERICAL. I AM NOT HYSTE
YSTERICAL. I AM NOT HYSTERICAL. I AM NOT HYSTERICAL. I AM NOT HYSTERICAL. I AM NOT HYSTERICAL. I AM NOT HYSTERICAL. I AM NOT HYST
HYSTERICAL. I AM NOT HYSTERICAL. I AM NOT HYSTERICAL. I AM NOT HYSTERICAL. I AM NOT HYSTERICAL. I AM NOT HYSTERICAL. I AM NOT
TERICAL. I AM NOT HYSTERICAL. I AM NOT HYSTERICAL. I AM NOT HYSTERICAL. I AM NOT HYSTERICAL. I AM NOT HYSTERICAL. I AM NOT HYST
ERICAL. I AM NOT HYSTERICAL. I AM NOT HYSTERICAL. I AM NOT HYSTERICAL. I AM NOT HYSTERICAL. I AM NOT HYSTERICAL. I AM NOT HYSTER
TERICAL. I AM NOT HYSTERICAL. I AM NOT HYSTERICAL. I AM NOT HYSTERICAL. I AM NOT HYSTERICAL. I AM NOT HYSTERICAL. I AM NOT HYSTE
TERICAL. I AM NOT HYSTERICAL. I AM NOT HYSTERICAL. I AM NOT HYSTERICAL. I AM NOT HYSTERICAL. I AM NOT HYSTERICAL. I AM NOT HYST
YSTERICAL. I AM NOT HYSTERICAL. I AM NOT HYSTERICAL. I AM NOT HYSTERICAL. I AM NOT HYSTERICAL. I AM NOT HYSTERICAL. I AM NOT HYS
ICAL. I AM NOT HYSTERICAL. I AM NOT HYSTERICAL. I AM NOT HYSTERICAL. I AM NOT HYSTERICAL. I AM NOT HYSTERICAL. I AM NOT HYSTERICAL.
YSTERICAL. I AM NOT HYSTERICAL. I AM NOT HYSTERICAL. I AM NOT HYSTERICAL. I AM NOT HYSTERICAL. I AM NOT HYSTERICAL. I AM NOT HYSTE
STERICAL. I AM NOT HYSTERICAL. I AM NOT HYSTERICAL. I AM NOT HYSTERICAL. I AM NOT HYSTERICAL. I AM NOT HYSTERICAL. I AM NOT HYSTE
HYSTERICAL. I AM NOT HYSTERICAL. I AM NOT HYSTERICAL. I AM NOT HYSTERICAL. I AM NOT HYSTERICAL. I AM NOT HYSTERICAL. I AM NOT HYS
YSTERICAL. I AM NOT HYSTERICAL. I AM NOT HYSTERICAL. I AM NOT HYSTERICAL. I AM NOT HYSTERICAL. I AM NOT HYSTERICAL. I AM NOT HYSTER
ERICAL. I AM NOT HYSTERICAL. I AM NOT HYSTERICAL. I AM NOT HYSTERICAL. I AM NOT HYSTERICAL. I AM NOT HYSTERICAL. I AM NOT HYSTER
TERICAL. I AM NOT HYSTERICAL. I AM NOT HYSTERICAL. I AM NOT HYSTERICAL. I AM NOT HYSTERICAL. I AM NOT HYSTERICAL. I AM NOT HYSTER
ERICAL. I AM NOT HYSTERICAL. I AM NOT HYSTERICAL. I AM NOT HYSTERICAL. I AM NOT HYSTERICAL. I AM NOT HYSTERICAL. I AM NOT HYSTERI
CAL. I AM NOT HYSTERICAL. I AM NOT HYSTERICAL. I AM NOT HYSTERICAL. I AM NOT HYSTERICAL. I AM NOT HYSTERICAL. I AM NOT HYSTERICAL.
RICAL. I AM NOT HYSTERICAL. I AM NOT HYSTERICAL. I AM NOT HYSTERICAL. I AM NOT HYSTERICAL. I AM NOT HYSTERICAL. I AM NOT HYSTERI
ERICAL. I AM NOT HYSTERICAL. I AM NOT HYSTERICAL. I AM NOT HYSTERICAL. I AM NOT HYSTERICAL. I AM NOT HYSTERICAL. I AM NOT HYSTER
TERICAL. I AM NOT HYSTERICAL. I AM NOT HYSTERICAL. I AM NOT HYSTERICAL. I AM NOT HYSTERICAL. I AM NOT HYSTERICAL. I AM NOT H
ERICAL. I AM NOT HYSTERICAL. I AM NOT HYSTERICAL. I AM NOT HYSTERICAL. I AM NOT HYSTERICAL. I AM NOT HYSTERICAL. I AM NOT HYSTER
ERICAL. I AM NOT HYSTERICAL. I AM NOT HYSTERICAL. I AM NOT HYSTERICAL. I AM NOT HYSTERICAL. I AM NOT HYSTERICAL. I AM NOT HYSTE
ERICAL. I AM NOT HYSTERICAL. I AM NOT HYSTERICAL. I AM NOT HYSTERICAL. I AM NOT HYSTERICAL. I AM NOT HYSTERICAL. I AM NOT HYST
RICAL. I AM NOT HYSTERICAL. I AM NOT HYSTERICAL. I AM NOT HYSTERICAL. I AM NOT HYSTERICAL. I AM NOT HYSTERICAL. I AM NOT HYSTE
RICAL. I AM NOT HYSTERICAL. I AM NOT HYSTERICAL. I AM NOT HYSTERICAL. I AM NOT HYSTERICAL. I AM NOT HYSTERICAL. I AM NOT HYSTER
RICAL. I AM NOT HYSTERICAL. I AM NOT HYSTERICAL. I AM NOT HYSTERICAL. I AM NOT HYSTERICAL. I AM NOT HYSTERICAL. I AM NOT HYSTERICAL.
ERICAL. I AM NOT HYSTERICAL. I AM NOT HYSTERICAL. I AM NOT HYSTERICAL. I AM NOT HYSTERICAL. I AM NOT HYSTERICAL. I AM NOT HYST
RICAL. I AM NOT HYSTERICAL. I AM NOT HYSTERICAL. I AM NOT HYSTERICAL. I AM NOT HYSTERICAL. I AM NOT HYSTERICAL. I AM NOT HYSTERICAL
RICAL. I AM NOT HYSTERICAL. I AM NOT HYSTERICAL. I AM NOT HYSTERICAL. I AM NOT HYSTERICAL. I AM NOT HYSTERICAL. I AM NOT HYSTERIC
RICAL. I AM NOT HYSTERICAL. I AM NOT HYSTERICAL. I AM NOT HYSTERICAL. I AM NOT HYSTERICAL. I AM NOT HYSTERICAL. I AM NOT HYST
ICAL. I AM NOT HYSTERICAL. I AM NOT HYSTERICAL. I AM NOT HYSTERICAL. I AM NOT HYSTERICAL. I AM NOT HYSTERICAL. I AM NOT HYS
CAL. I AM NOT HYSTERICAL. I AM NOT HYSTERICAL. I AM NOT HYSTERICAL. I AM NOT HYSTERICAL. I AM NOT HYSTERICAL. I AM NOT HYSTERIC
RICAL. I AM NOT HYSTERICAL. I AM NOT HYSTERICAL. I AM NOT HYSTERICAL. I AM NOT HYSTERICAL. I AM NOT HYSTERICAL. I AM NOT HYSTERI
ERICAL. I AM NOT HYSTERICAL. I AM NOT HYSTERICAL. I AM NOT HYSTERICAL. I AM NOT HYSTERICAL. I AM NOT HYSTERICAL. I AM NOT HYSTER
RICAL. I AM NOT HYSTERICAL. I AM NOT HYSTERICAL. I AM NOT HYSTERICAL. I AM NOT HYSTERICAL. I AM NOT HYSTERICAL. I AM NOT HYSTE
RICAL. I AM NOT HYSTERICAL. I AM NOT HYSTERICAL. I AM NOT HYSTERICAL. I AM NOT HYSTERICAL. I AM NOT HYSTERICAL. I AM NOT HYSTERICAL
ICAL. I AM NOT HYSTERICAL. I AM NOT HYSTERICAL. I AM NOT HYSTERICAL. I AM NOT HYSTERICAL. I AM NOT HYSTERICAL. I AM NOT HYSTER
RICAL. I AM NOT HYSTERICAL. I AM NOT HYSTERICAL. I AM NOT HYSTERICAL. I AM NOT HYSTERICAL. I AM NOT HYSTERICAL. I AM NOT HYSTE
RICAL. I AM NOT HYSTERICAL. I AM NOT HYSTERICAL. I AM NOT HYSTERICAL. I AM NOT HYSTERICAL. I AM NOT HYSTERICAL. I AM NOT HYSTERICAL

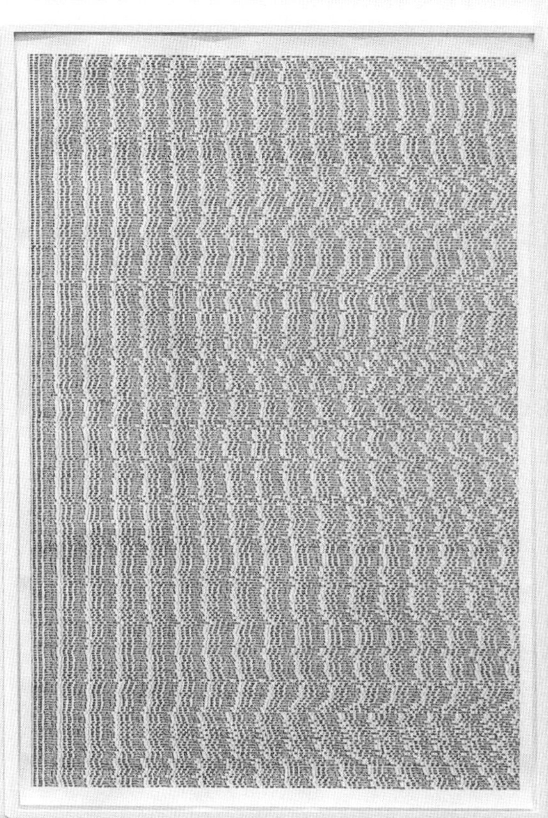

S E L B S T

KRITIK

PRIVILEGED

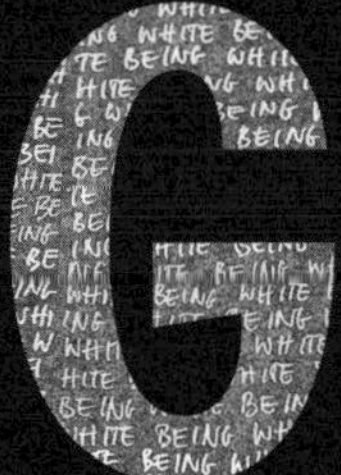

bungen. Die Aufwertung des Eigenen ist immer gekoppelt an die Abwertung des Anderen, das ist im Grunde ein- und dieselbe Operation. So, wie das Zeichnen auf dem Kohlepapier gleichzeitig die Zeichnung darauf und den Abrieb auf dem darunterliegenden Papier erzeugt. ‚BEING WHITE' erschöpft sich dabei aus meiner Sicht aber nicht im kolonialen Hautfarbenrassismus, sondern schließt ein ganzes Repertoire an kulturellen, religiösen, ökonomischen und sozialen Charakteristika ein, die zunehmend wieder Unterdrückung, Ausbeutung oder – aktuell – Abschottung legitimieren sollen. So wird umgekehrt ‚BEING WHITE' zu etwas, wofür man sich auch schämen kann. ..."

"... 'BEING WHITE' naturally refers to the whole complex of issues from exclusion to attributions. The upvaluation of oneself is always coupled with a devaluation of others, in principle it is one and the same operation. Just as the act of drawing on the carbon paper simultaneously generates the drawing on its surface and the tracing on the paper beneath. However, in my view 'BEING WHITE' does not just address the colonial racism of skin color. Instead it includes a whole repertoire of cultural, religious, economic and social characteristics which once again are being increasingly used to legitimize suppression, exploitation, or—currently—isolation. Thus, conversely, 'BEING WHITE' is something which one can also be ashamed of. ..."

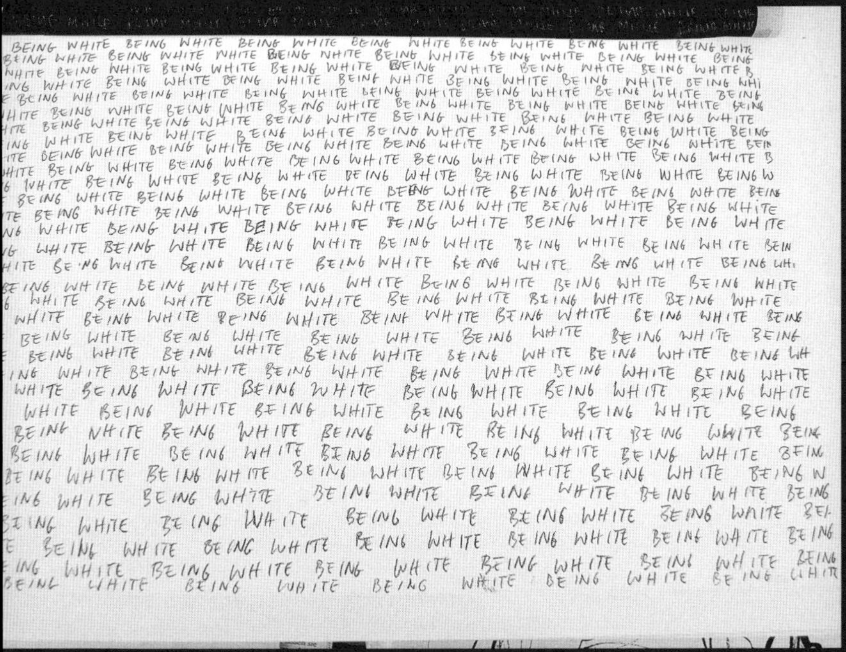

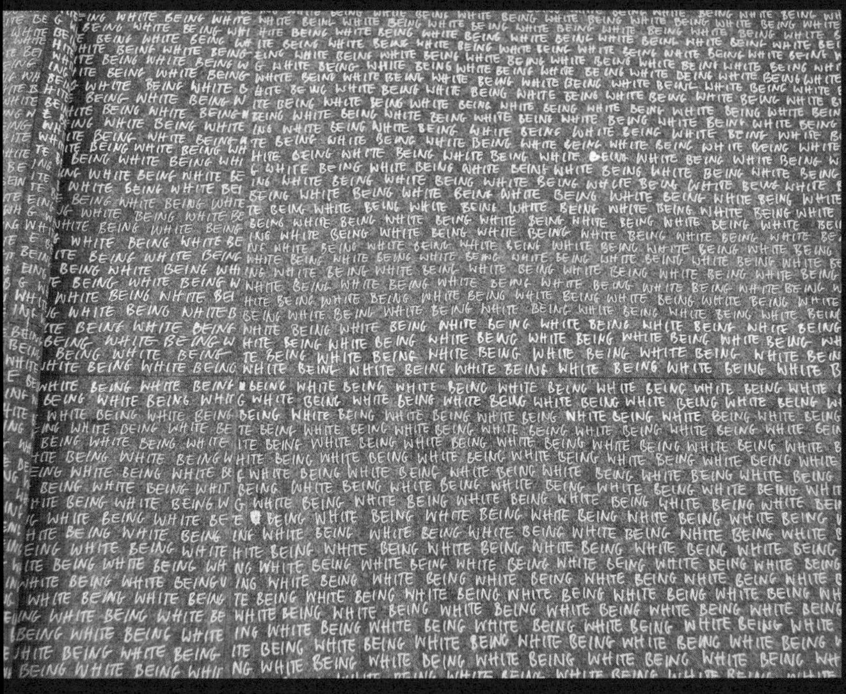

WHITE BEING WHITE BEING WHITE BEING WHITE BEING WHITE BEING WHITE BEING WHITE BEING WHITE BEING WHITE BEING WHITE BEING WHITE BEING WHITE BEING WHITE BEING WHITE BEING

WHITE BEING WHITE BEING WHITE BEING WHITE BEING WHITE BEING WHITE BEING WHITE BEING WHITE BEING
WHITE BEING WHITE BEING WHITE BEING WHITE BEING WHITE BEING WHITE BEING WHITE BEING WHITE BEING
WHITE BEING WHITE BEING WHITE BEING WHITE BEING WHITE BEING WHITE BEING WHITE BEING WHITE BEING
WHITE BEING WHITE BEING WHITE BEING WHITE BEING WHITE BEING WHITE BEING WHITE BEING WHITE BEING
WHITE BEING WHITE BEING WHITE BEING WHITE BEING WHITE BEING WHITE BEING WHITE BEING WHITE BEING
WHITE BEING WHITE BEING WHITE BEING WHITE BEING WHITE BEING WHITE BEING WHITE BEING WHITE BEING
WHITE BEING WHITE BEING WHITE BEING WHITE BEING WHITE BEING WHITE BEING WHITE BEING WHITE BEING
WHITE BEING WHITE BEING WHITE BEING WHITE BEING WHITE BEING WHITE BEING WHITE BEING WHITE BEING
WHITE BEING WHITE BEING WHITE BEING WHITE BEING WHITE BEING WHITE BEING WHITE BEING WHITE BEING
WHITE BEING WHITE BEING WHITE BEING WHITE BEING WHITE BEING WHITE BEING WHITE BEING WHITE BEING
WHITE BEING WHITE BEING WHITE BEING WHITE BEING WHITE BEING WHITE BEING WHITE BEING WHITE BEING
WHITE BEING WHITE BEING WHITE BEING WHITE BEING WHITE BEING WHITE BEING WHITE BEING WHITE BEING

BEING WHITE BEING WHITE BEING WHITE BEING WHITE BEING WHITE BEING WHITE BEING WHITE BEING WHITE BEING WHITE BEING WHITE BEING WHITE BEING WHITE
BEING WHITE BEING WHITE BEING WHITE BEING WHITE BEING WHITE BEING WHITE BEING WHITE BEING WHITE BEING WHITE BEING WHITE BEING WHITE BEING WHITE
BEING WHITE BEING WHITE BEING WHITE BEING WHITE BEING WHITE BEING WHITE BEING WHITE BEING WHITE BEING WHITE BEING WHITE BEING WHITE BEING WHITE
BEING WHITE BEING WHITE BEING WHITE BEING WHITE BEING WHITE BEING WHITE BEING WHITE BEING WHITE BEING WHITE BEING WHITE BEING WHITE BEING WHITE
BEING WHITE BEING WHITE BEING WHITE BEING WHITE BEING WHITE BEING WHITE BEING WHITE BEING WHITE BEING WHITE BEING WHITE BEING WHITE BEING WHITE
BEING WHITE BEING WHITE BEING WHITE BEING WHITE BEING WHITE BEING WHITE BEING WHITE BEING WHITE BEING WHITE BEING WHITE BEING WHITE BEING WHITE

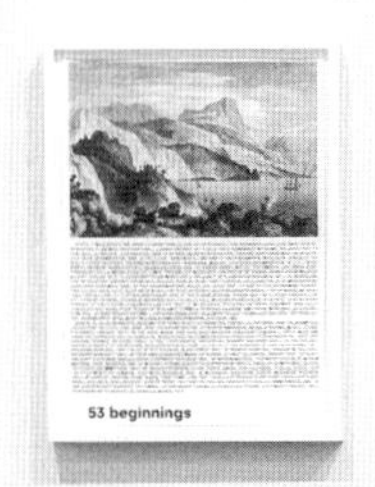
53 beginnings

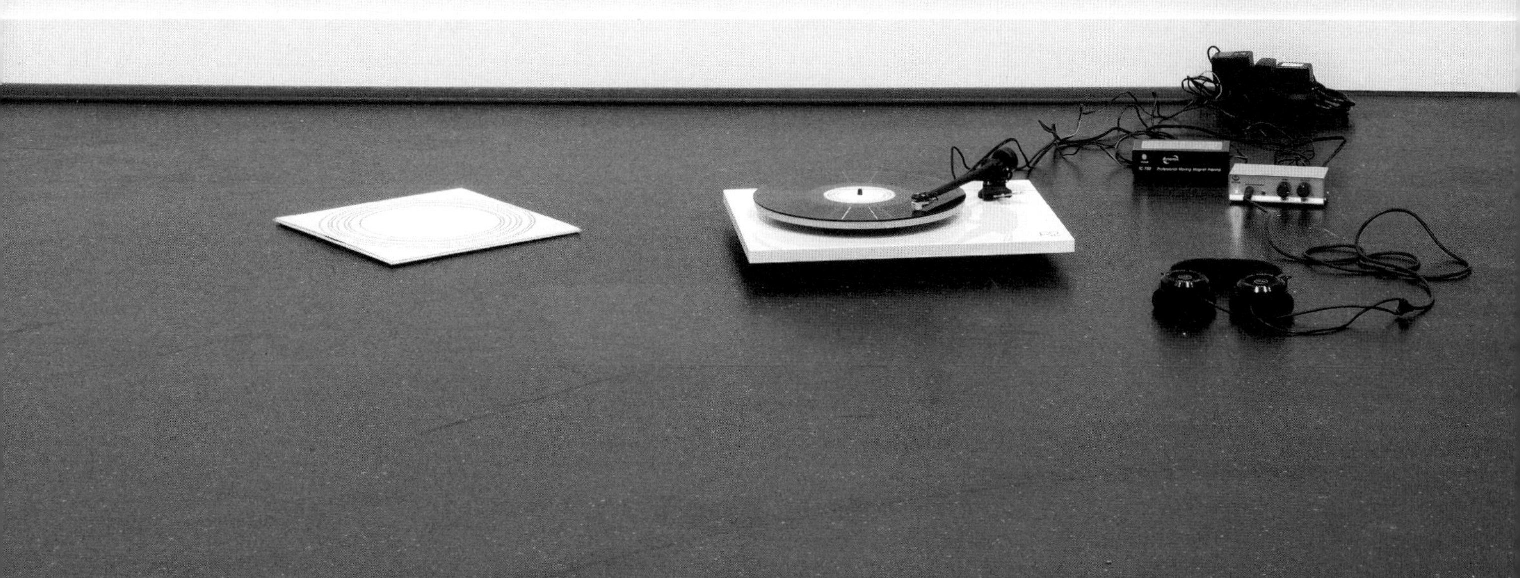

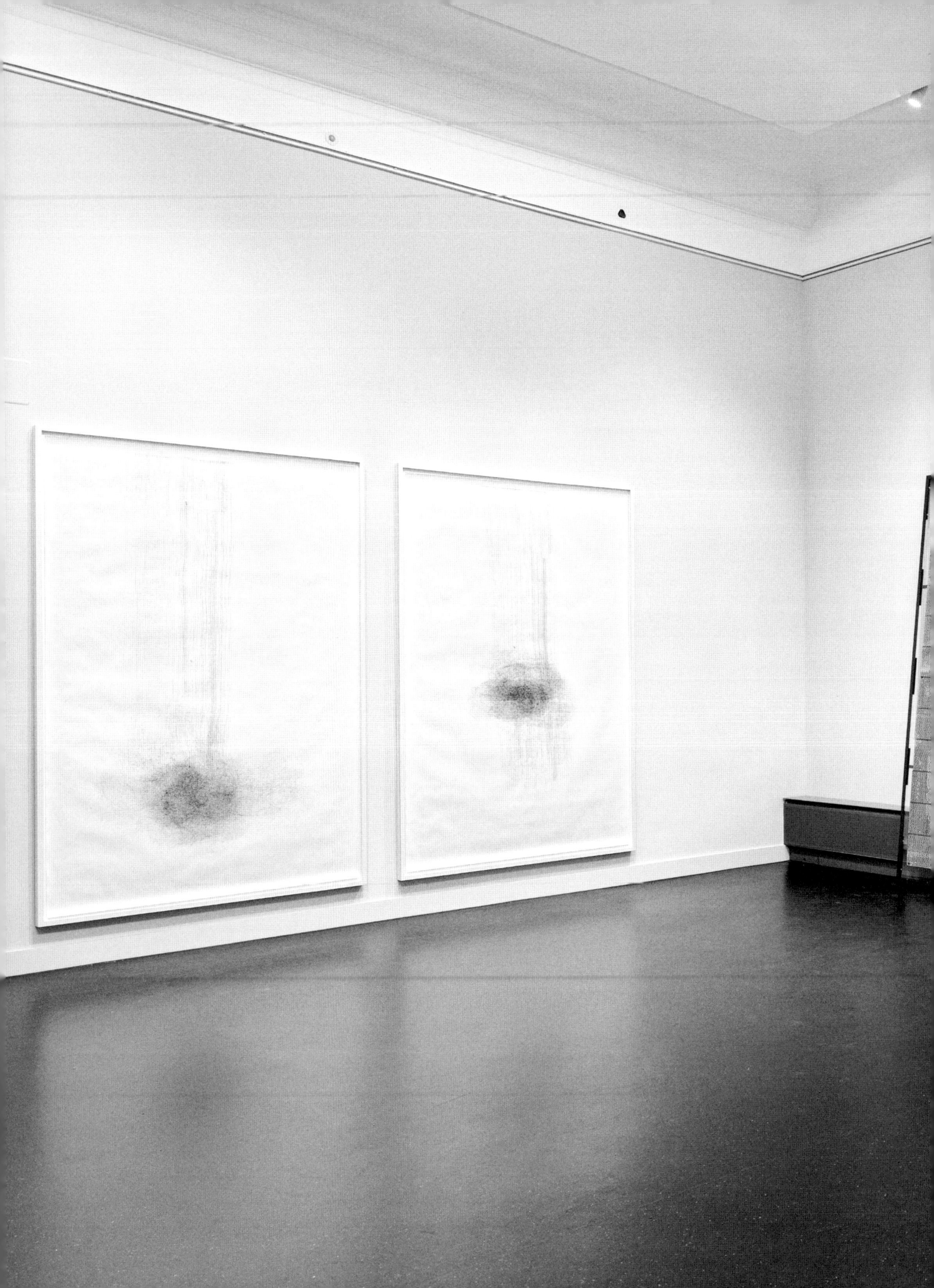

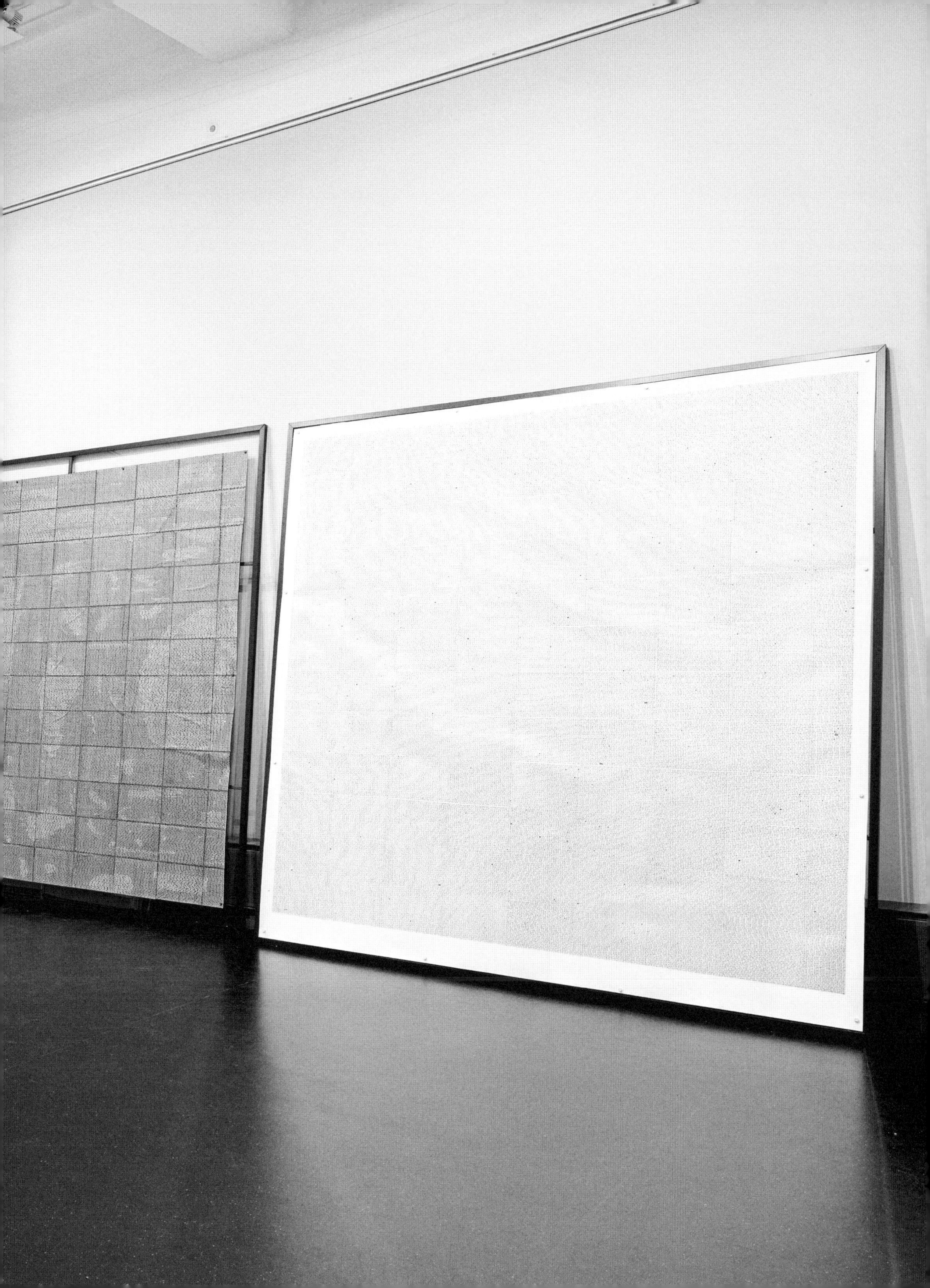

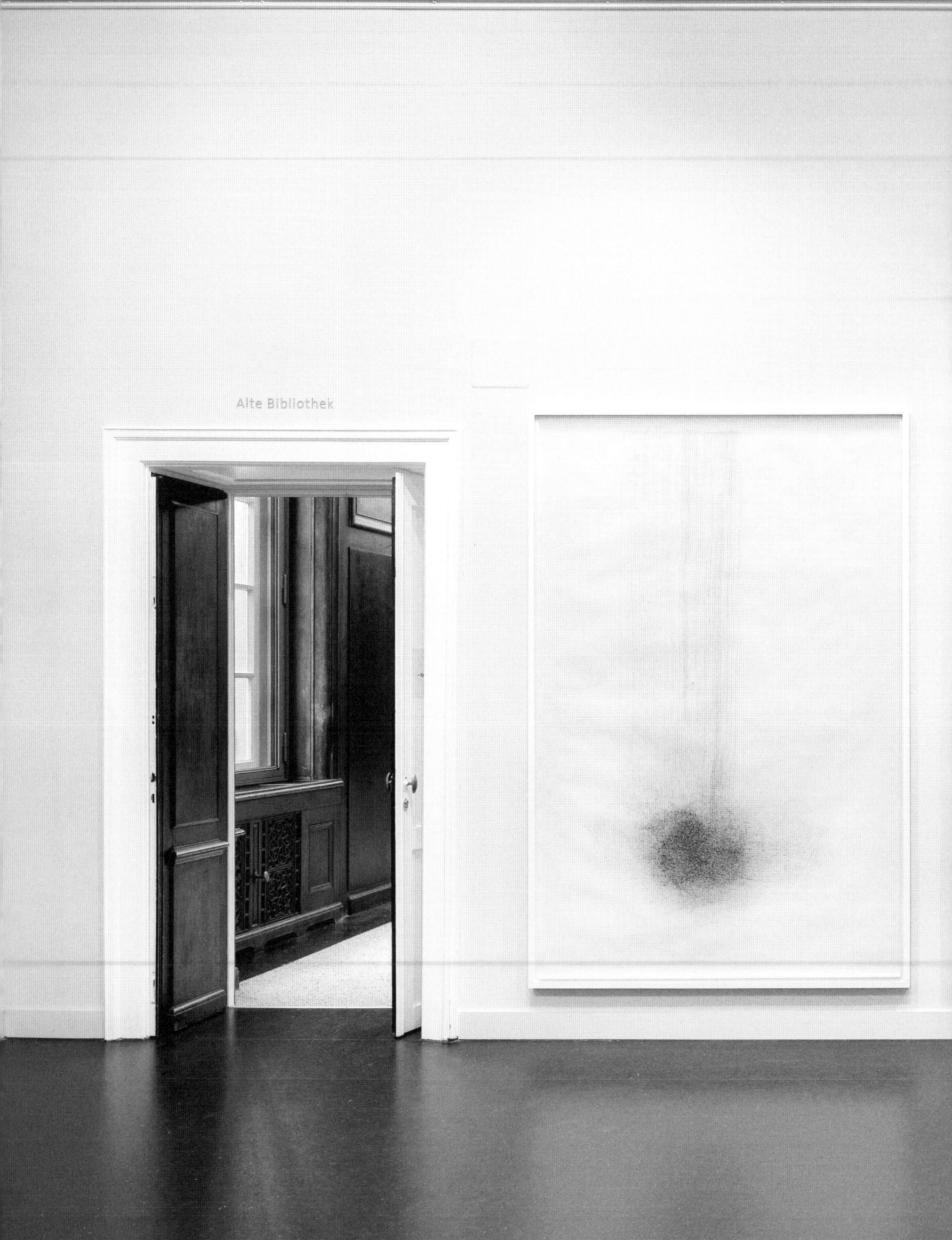
Alte Bibliothek

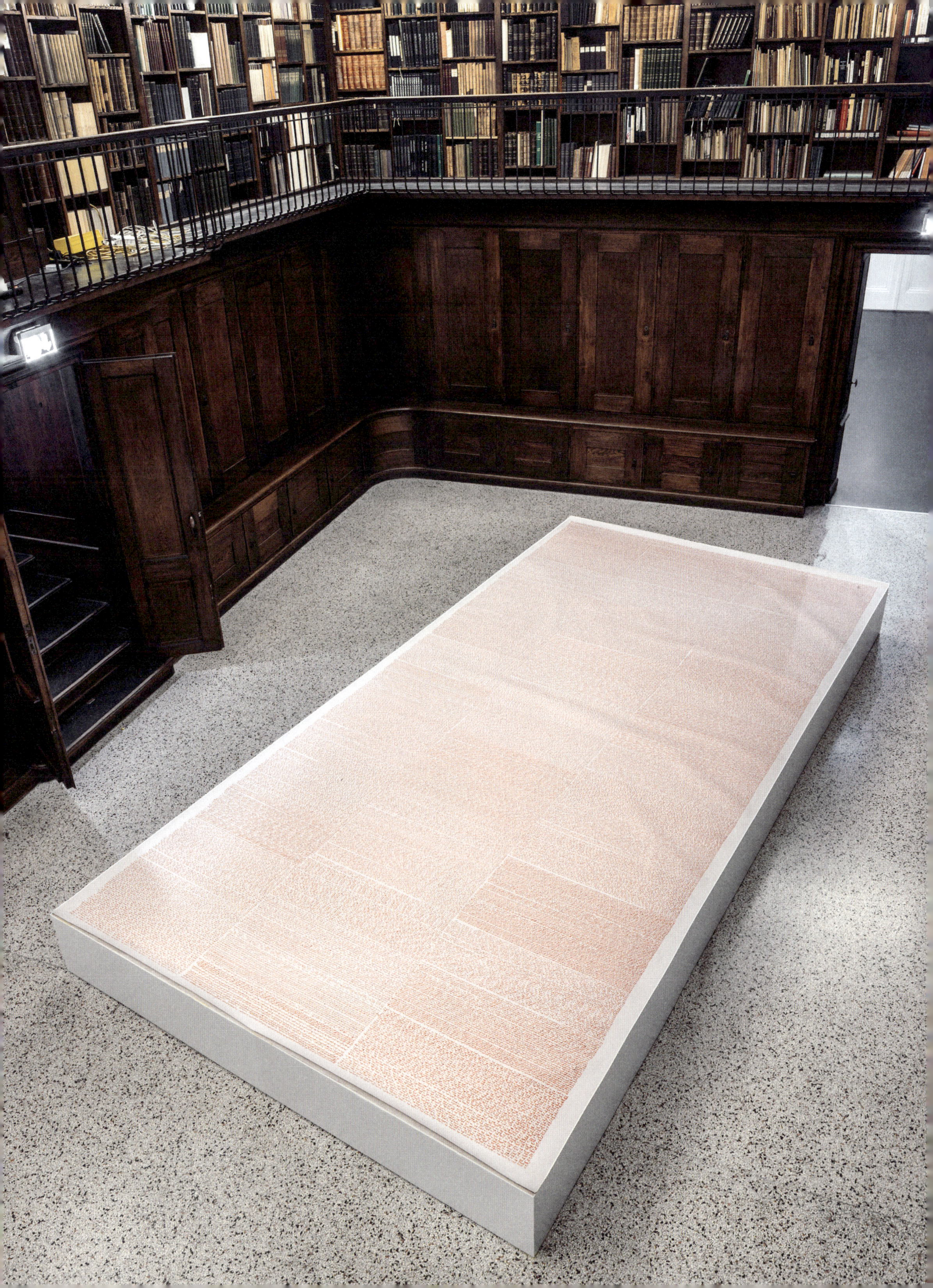

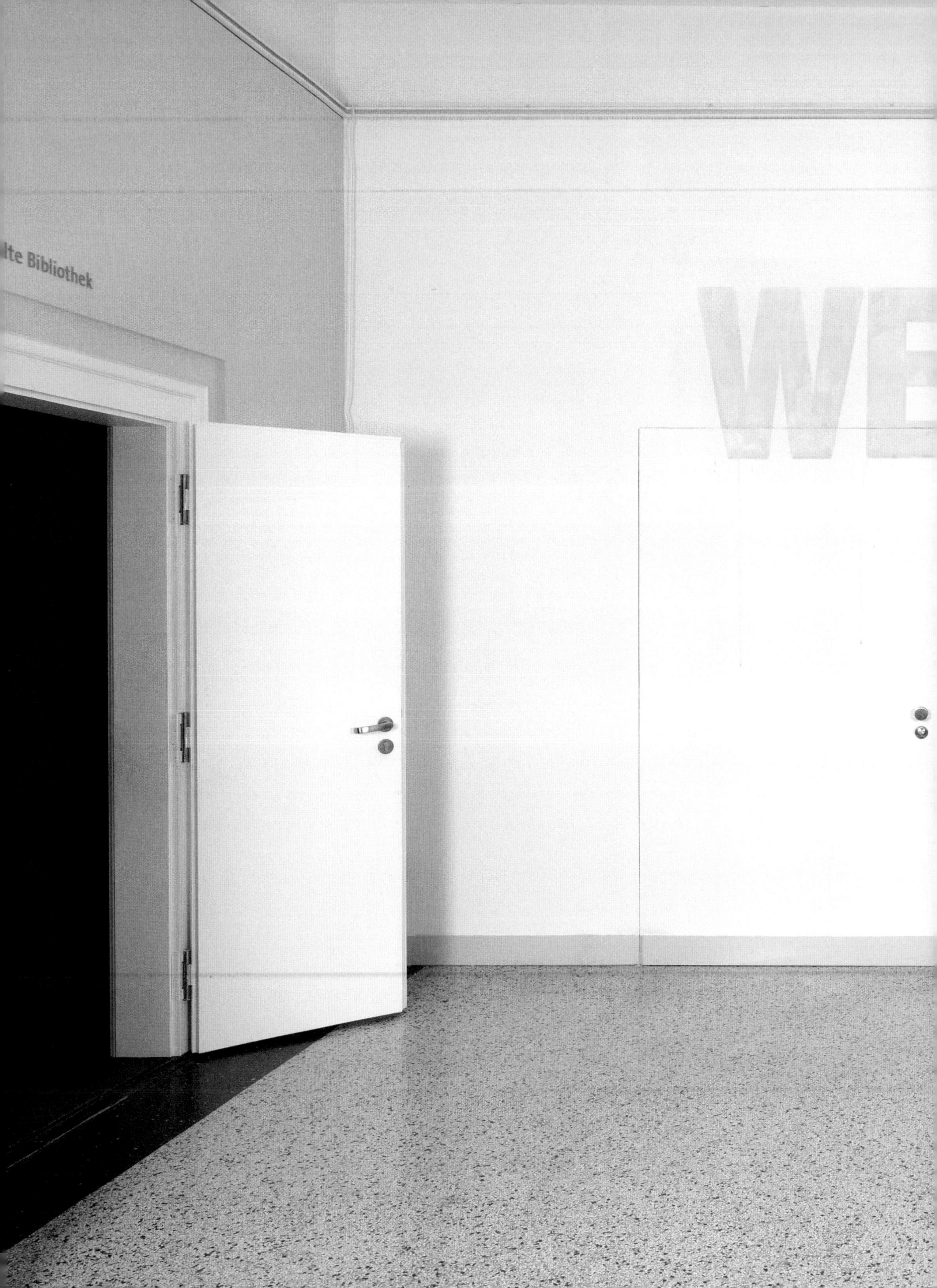
lte Bibliothek

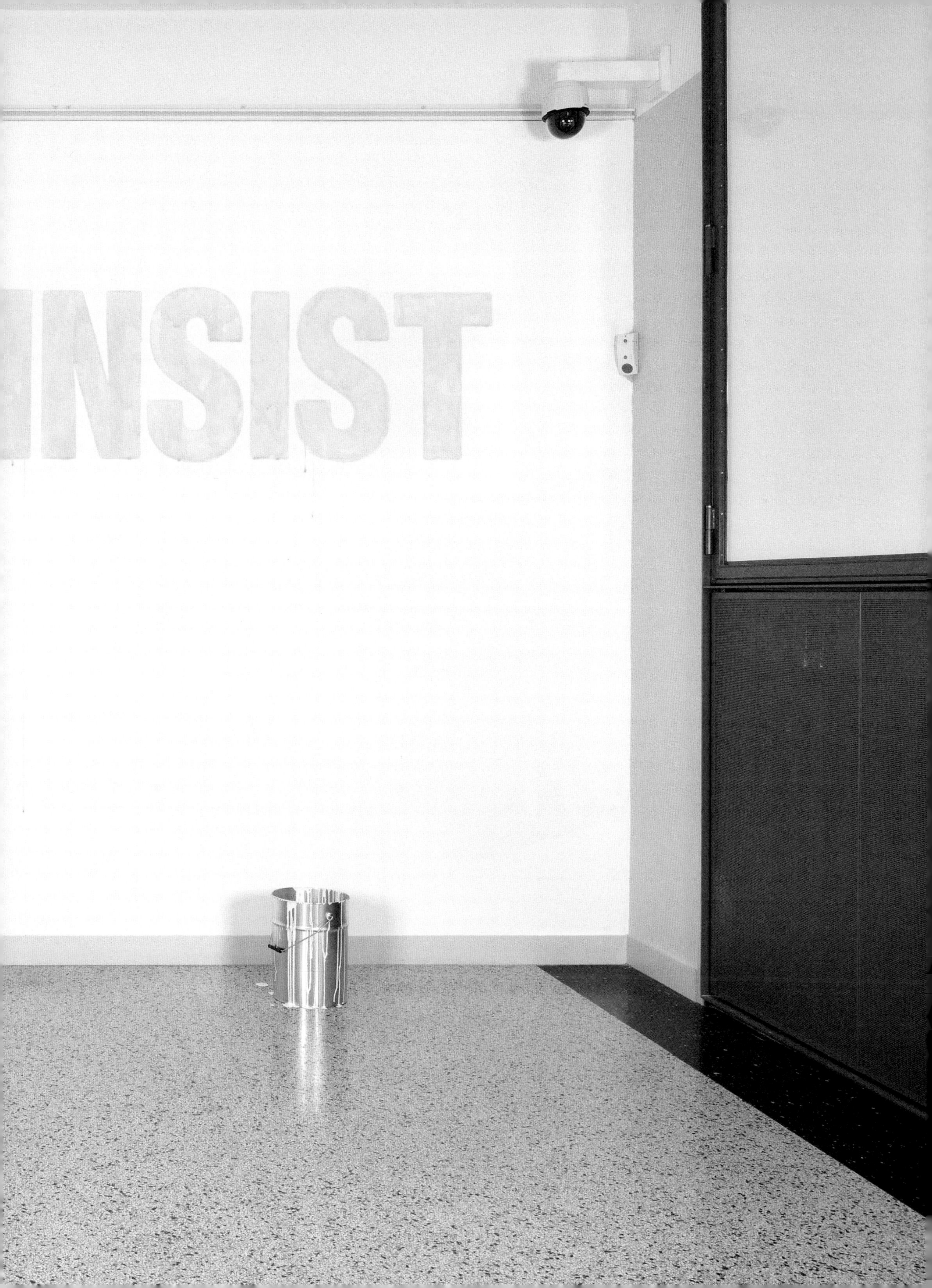
INSIST

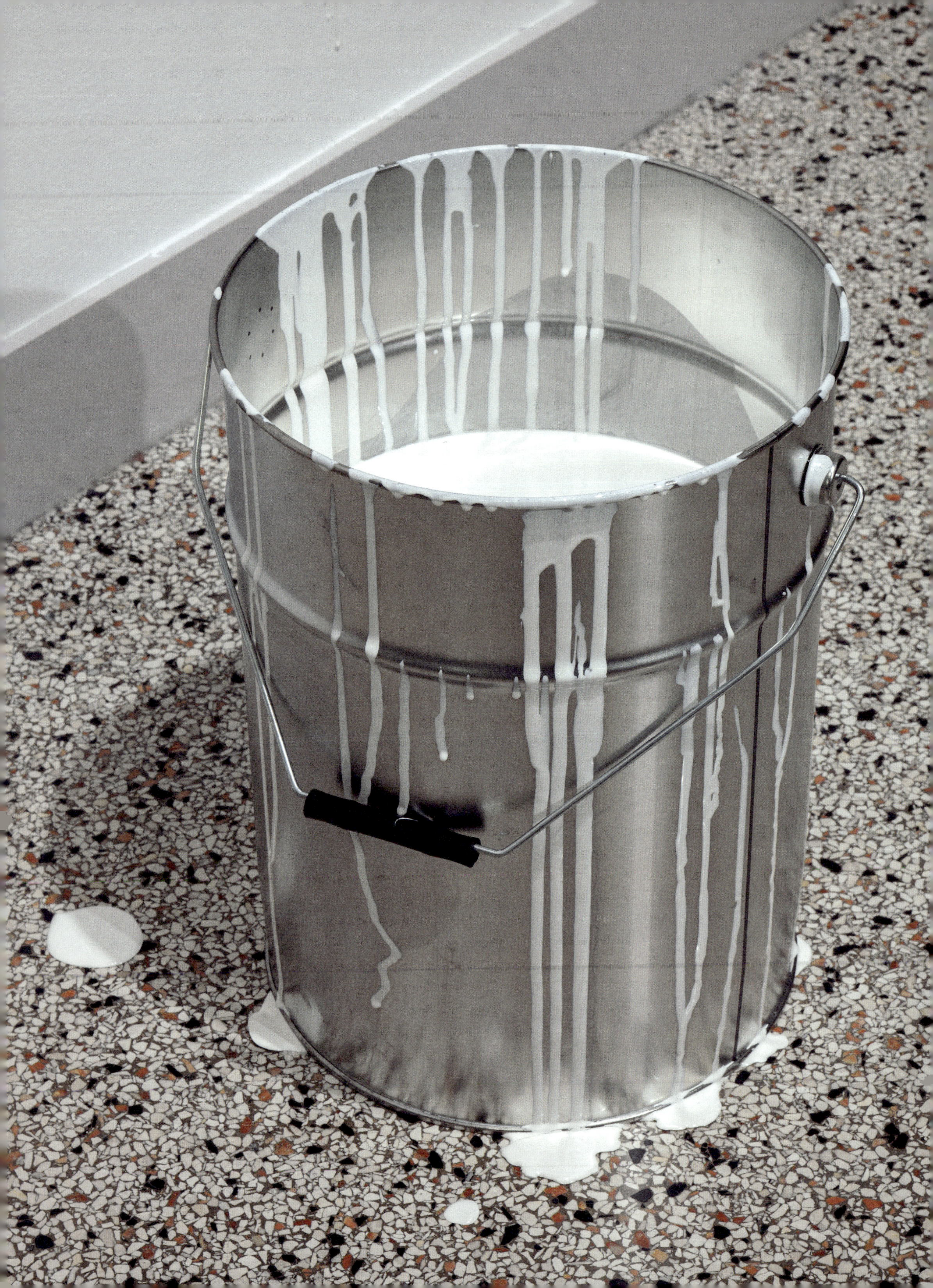

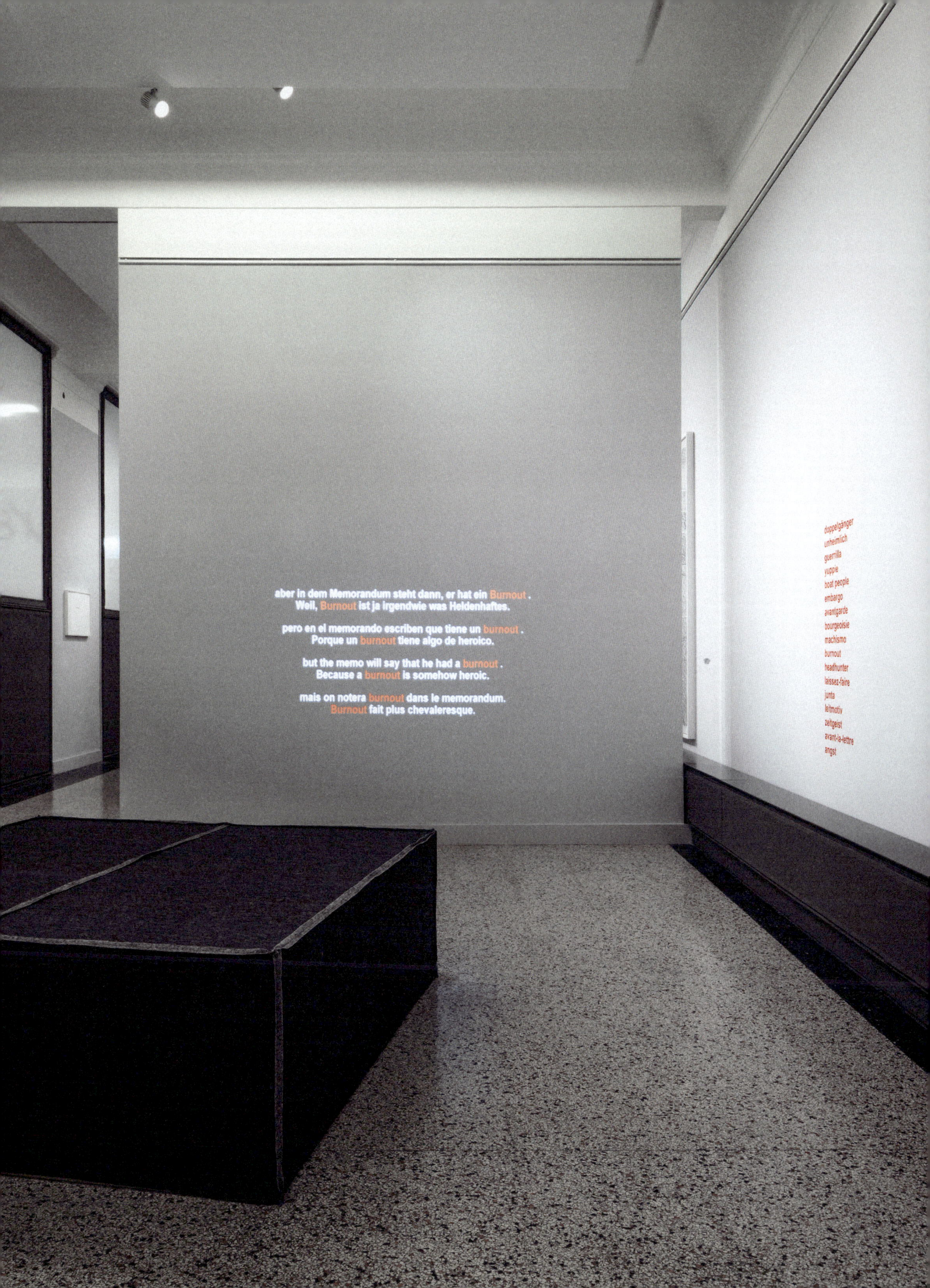
aber in dem Memorandum steht dann, er hat ein Burnout .
Weil, Burnout ist ja irgendwie was Heldenhaftes.
pero en el memorando escriben que tiene un burnout .
Porque un burnout tiene algo de heroico.
but the memo will say that he had a burnout .
Because a burnout is somehow heroic.
mais on notera burnout dans le memorandum.
Burnout fait plus chevaleresque.
doppelgänger
unheimlich
guerrilla
yuppie
boat people
embargo
avantgarde
bourgeoisie
machismo
burnout
headhunter
laissez-faire
junta
leitmotiv
zeitgeist
avant-la-lettre
angst

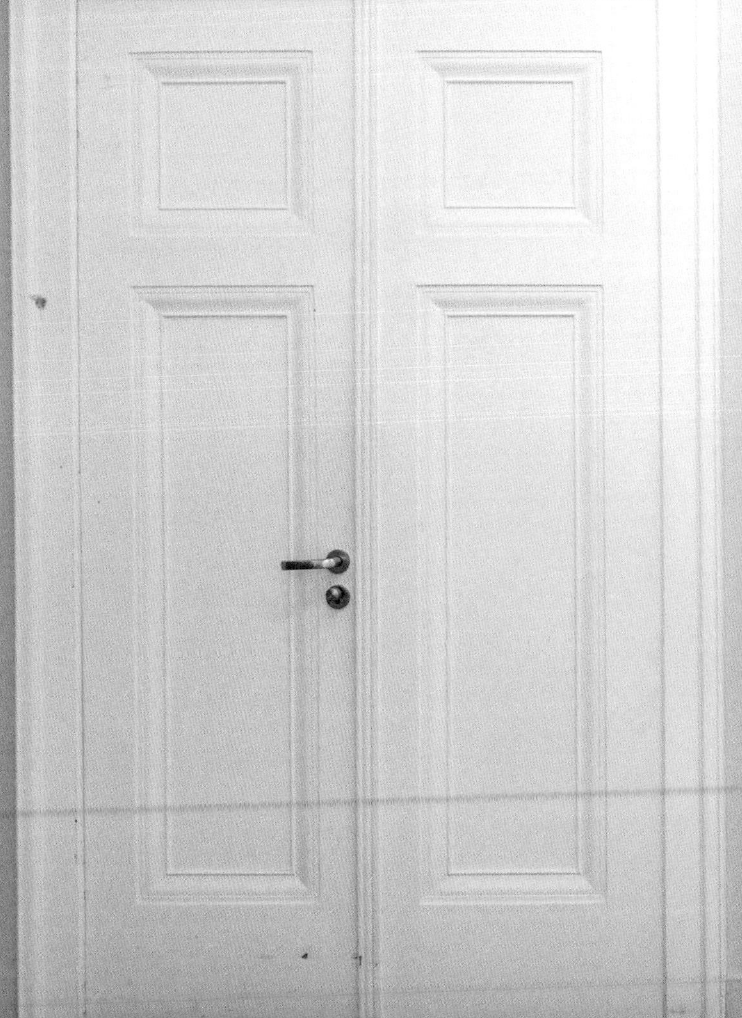
FOTOGRAFIEREN VERBOTEN
photography prohibited

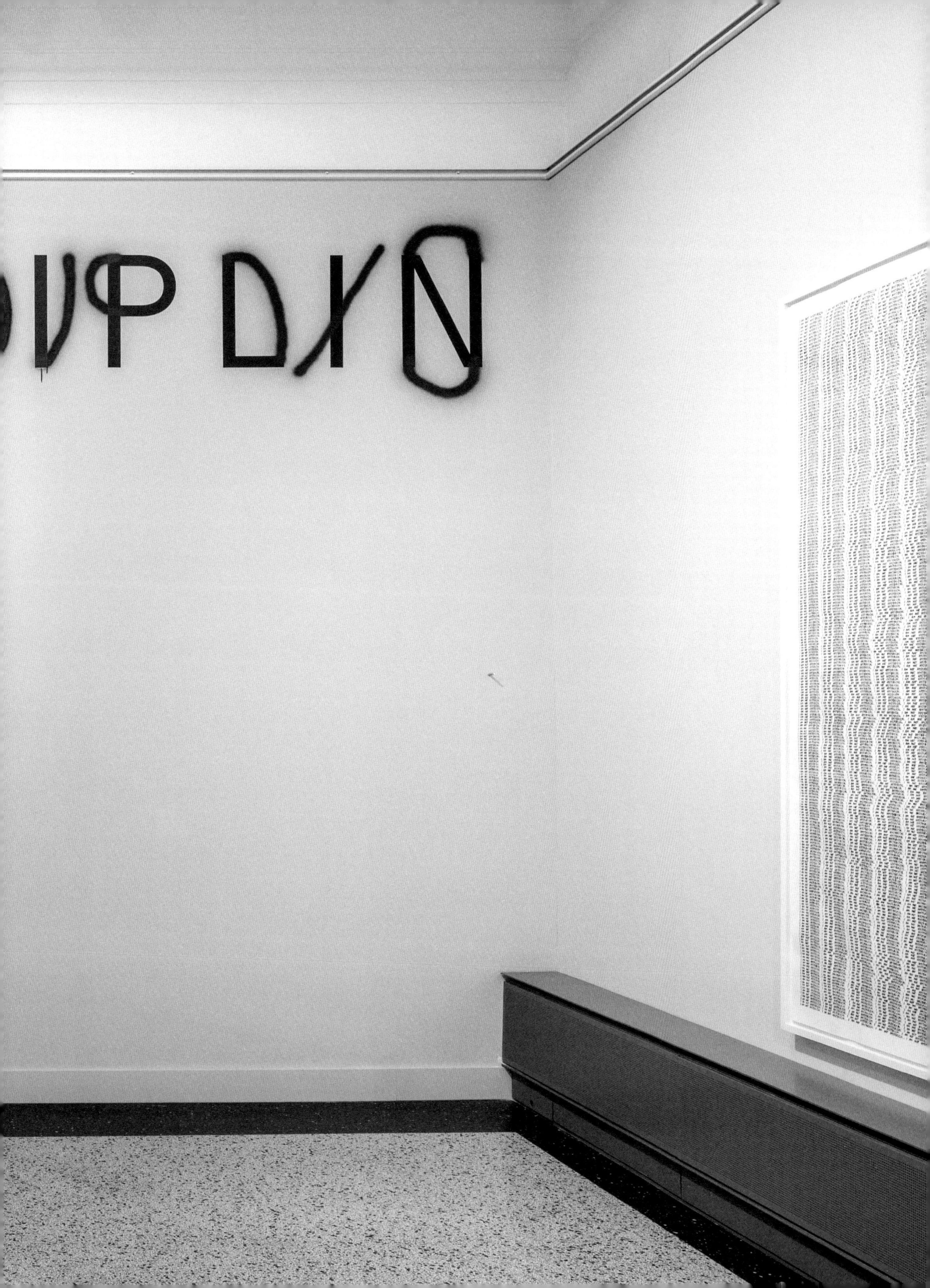

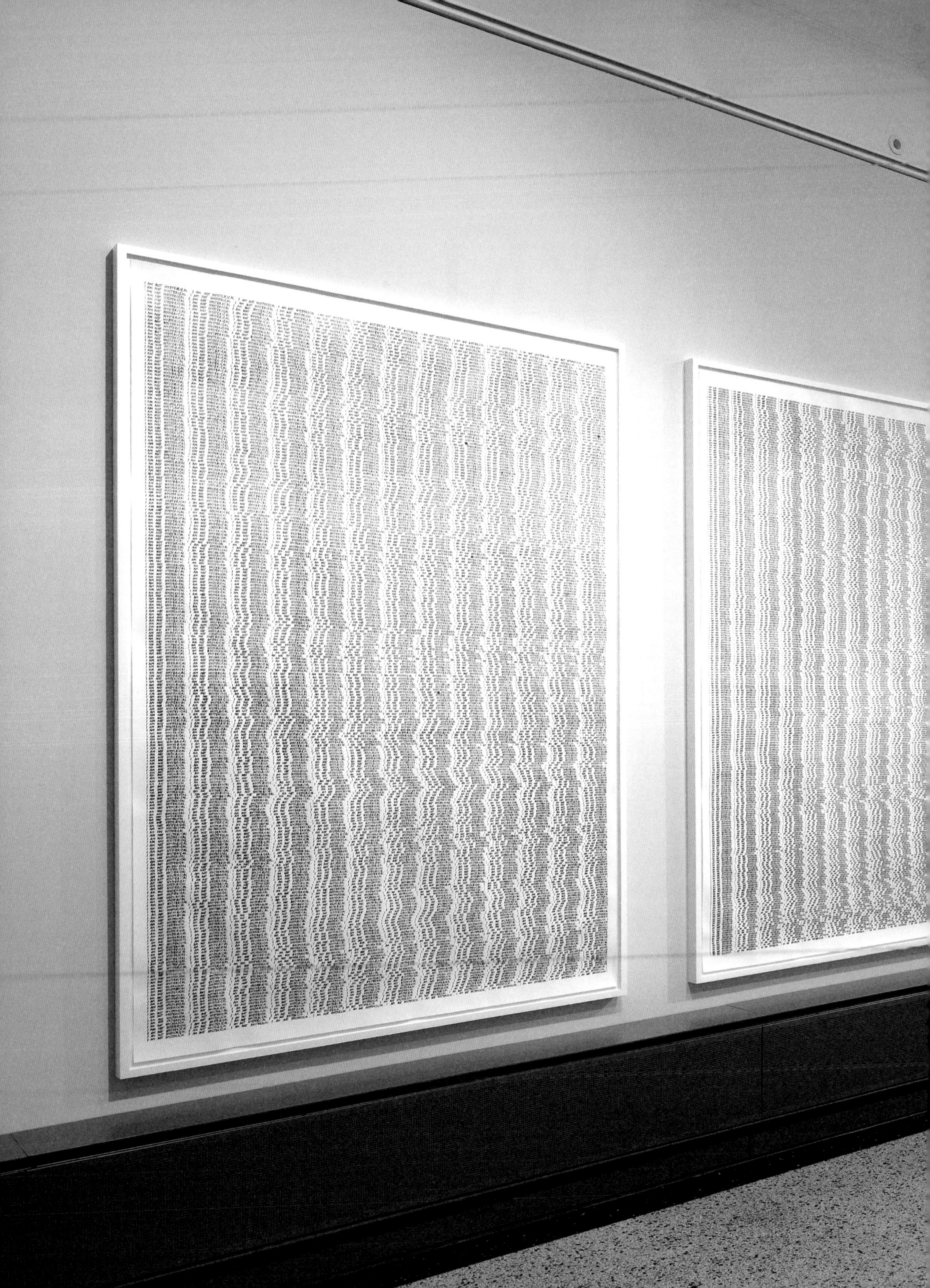
I AM NOT HYSTERICAL

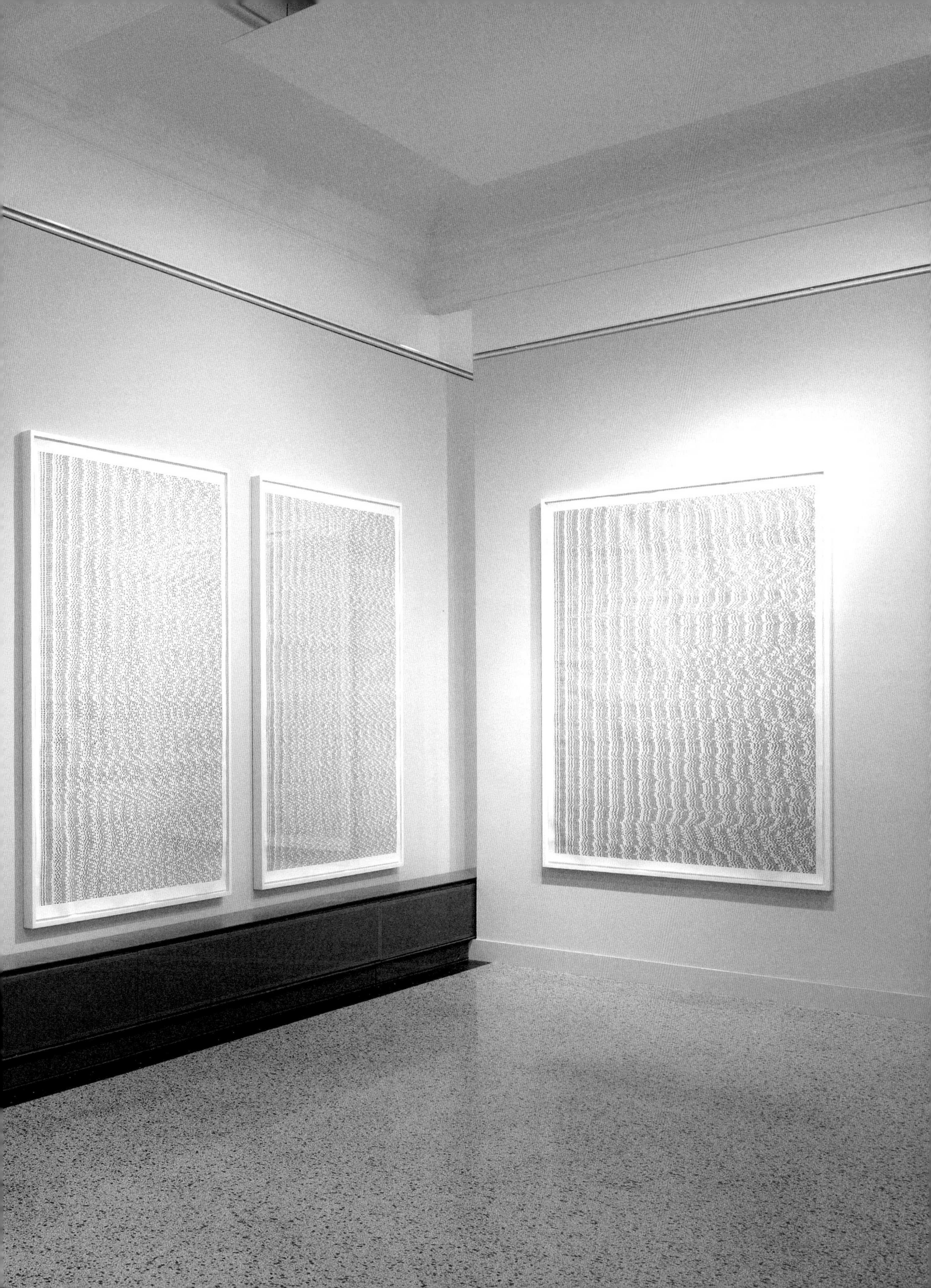

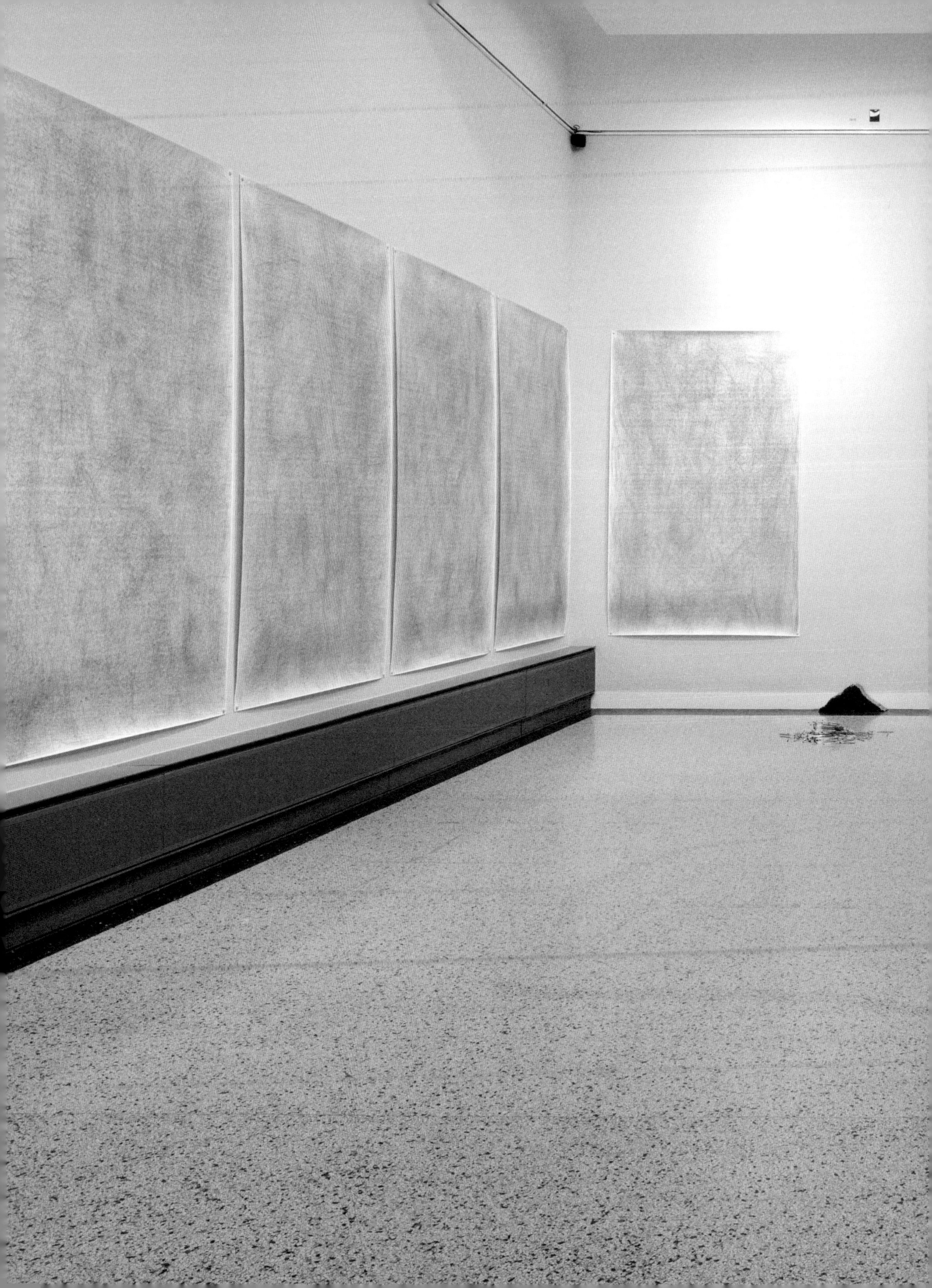

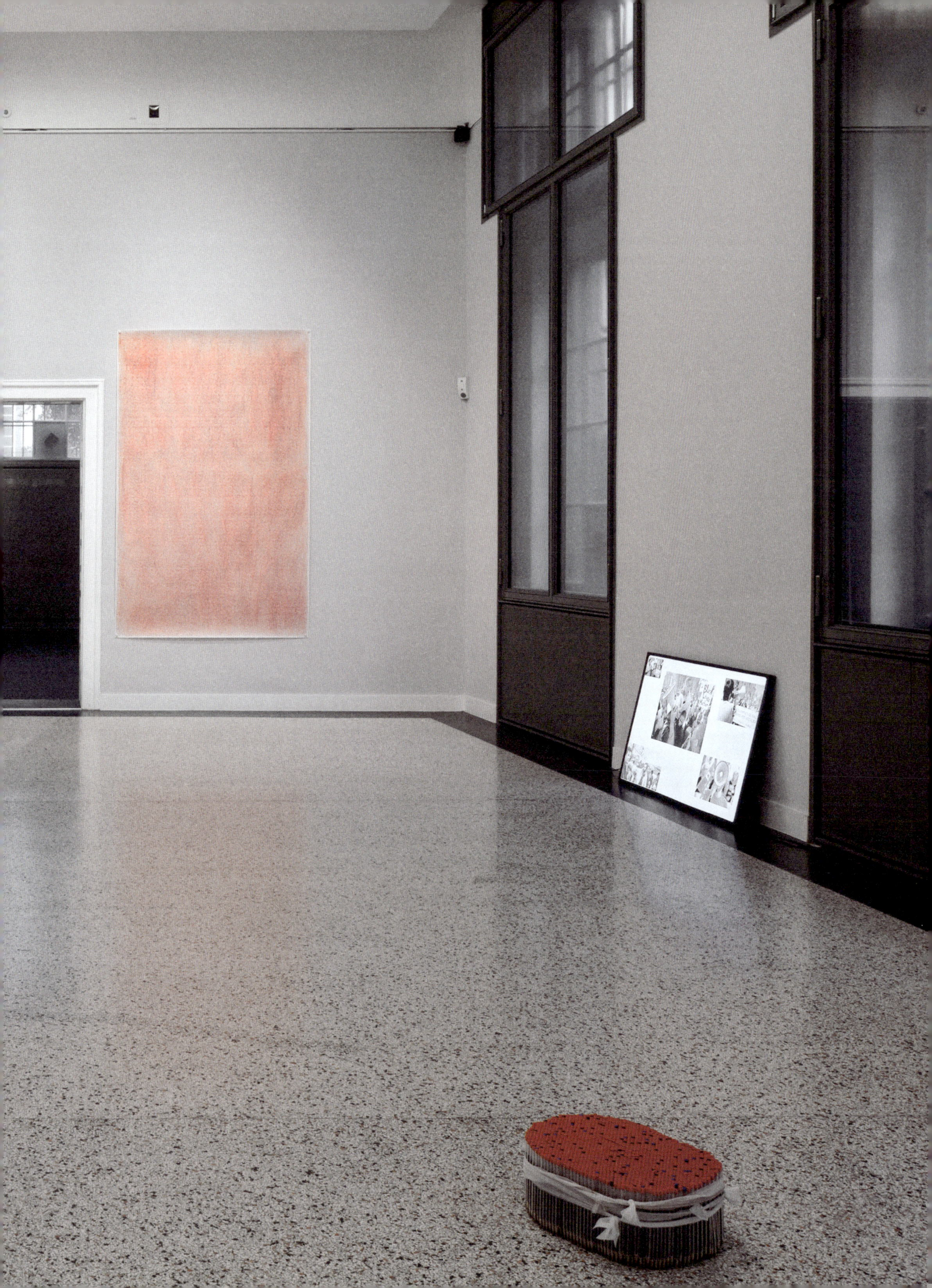

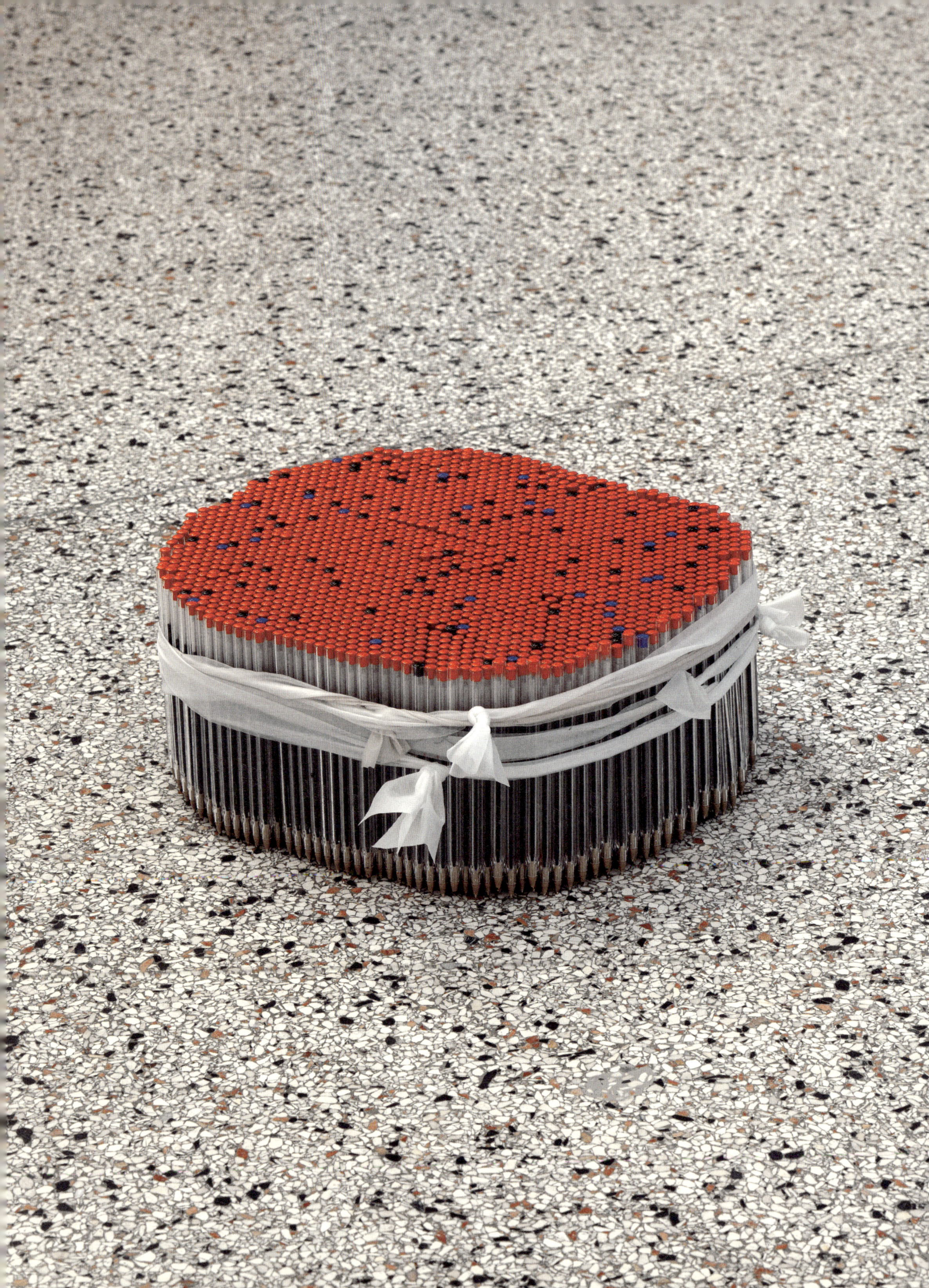

MELANCHOLIA

 Melancholia **2015/16** Tusche auf Papier **ink on paper** **550 × 271 cm**

blue I'm feeling blue I'm feeling blue I'm feeling
I'm feeling blue I'm feeling blue I'm feeling blue
lue I'm feeling blue I'm feeling blue I'm feeling
blue I'm feeling blue I'm feeling blue I'm feeling
eeling blue I'm feeling blue I'm feeling blue I'm
blue I'm feeling blue I'm feeling blue I'm feeling
blue I'm feelingblue I'm feeling blue I'm feelingblue
I'm feeling blue I'm feeling blue I'm feeling blue
blue I'm feeling blue I'm feeling blue I'm feeling blue
I'm feeling blue I'm feeling blue I'm feeling blue I'm
blue I'm feeling blue I'm feeling blue I'm feeling

e I'm feelingblue I'm feeling blue I'm feeling blue
eeling blue I'm feeling blue I'm feelingblue I'm feeling
ling blue I'm feelingblue I'm feeling blue I'm fee-
blue I'm feeling blue I'm feeling blue I'm feeling blue

I'm feeling blue I'm feelingblue I'm feelingblue I'm
g blue I'm feeling blue I'm feeling blue I'm feeling

I'mfeelingblue
blue I'mfeel
blue I'mfeeling
blue I'mfeelin
blue I'mfeelin
blue I'mfeeling
blue I'm feel
I'mfeelingbl
I'mfeelingblue,
blue I'mfeelin
blue I'mfeelin
I'mfeelingblue.
feelingblue I'mf
lingblue I'mf
blue I'mfeeling
feelingblue I'm

CLOSE READING

doppelgänger
unheimlich
guerrilla
yuppie
boat people
embargo
avantgarde
bourgeoisie
machismo
burnout
headhunter
laissez-faire
junta
leitmotiv
zeitgeist
avant-la-lettre
angst

 close reading 2013 Video 47:50 min

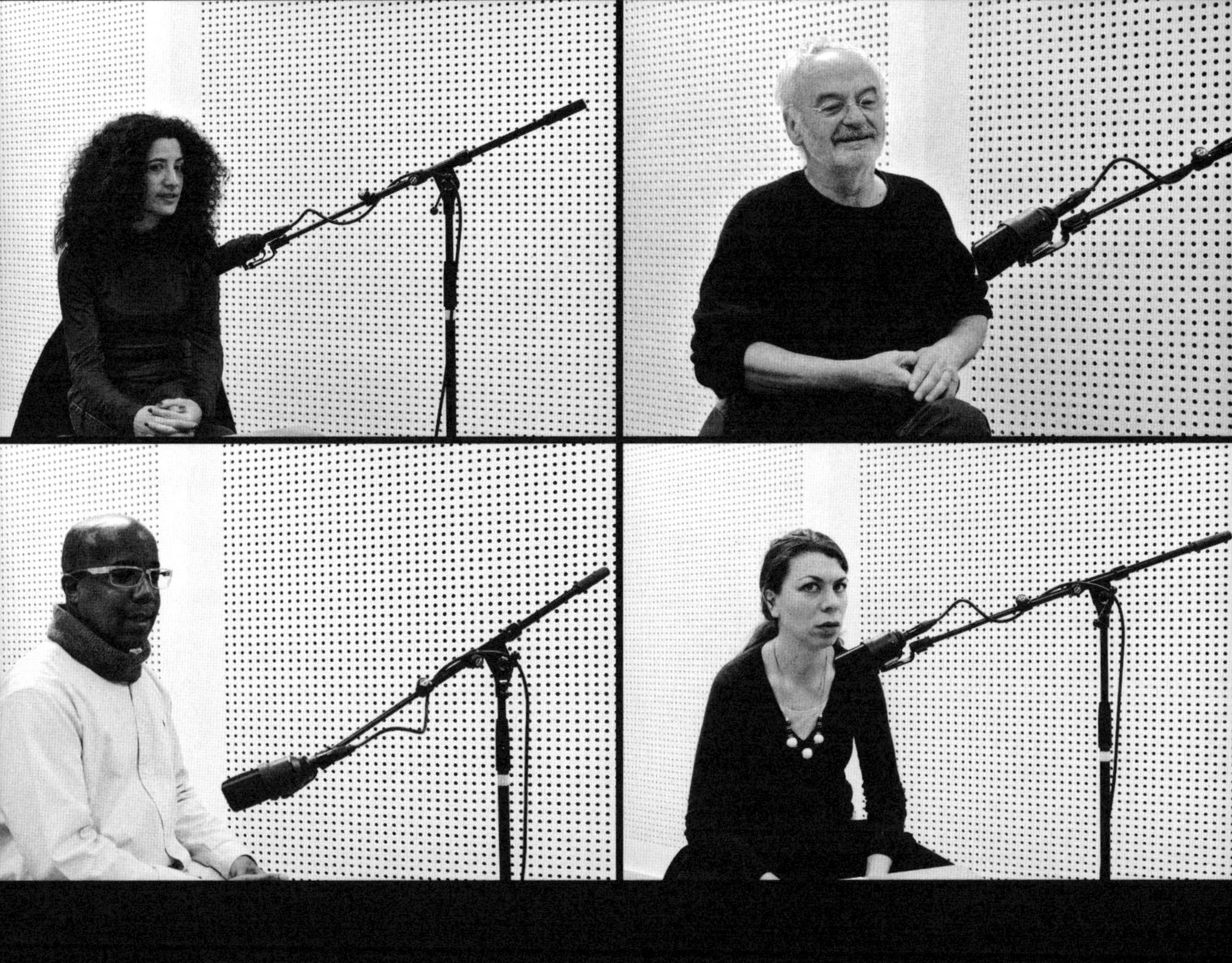

„… Worte wandern ebenso wie Menschen von einer Sprache, von einer Kultur oder einem Land in das andere und bringen dabei etwas mit, was sich nicht ohne Rest in das neue Umfeld übersetzen lässt. Neologismen sind Begriffe, die unübersetzt von der einen Sprache in die andere ziehen und als Fremde etwas Selbstverständliches bekommen. Dass die Erklärung solcher Begriffe mitunter etwas mehr Mühe bedeutet, als die, die ganz der eigenen Sprache angehören, macht die Tonspur dieses Films immer wieder spürbar. Aber auch, dass dieser Aufwand sich lohnt. …“

"… Just like people words can migrate from one language, from a culture or a country, to another, bringing something with them which cannot be completely translated in the new environment. Neologisms are terms which move from one language to another untranslated, and as aliens are eventually taken for granted. The sound track of this film repeatedly makes it clear that the explanation of such terms sometimes requires more effort than that required for those terms which are an integral part of the language. But also the fact that this effort is worth it. …"

doppelgänger
unheimlich
guerrilla
yuppie
boat people
embargo
avantgarde
bourgeoisie
machismo
burnout
headhunter
laissez-faire
junta
leitmotiv
zeitgeist
avant-la-lettre
angst

Es gibt eine fließende Grenze von der Guerilla zum Terrorismus,

Il existe une frontière flottante entre guérilla et terrorisme,

There's a gray area between guerrilla warfare and terrorism,

Hay un límite borroso entre guerrilla y terrorismo,

---

wobei ich sagen würde,
der Begriff Guerilla sollte und ist meist auch denen vorbehalten,

même si je dirais que le terme de guérilla est souvent réservé à ceux

although I would say that the term guerrilla
should be and usually is reserved for those

donde yo diría que el término guerrilla debería,
y la mayoría de las veces se mantiene

---

die aus legitimen

qui combattent pour des raisons légitimes,

who have legitimate

para aquellos que luchan por razones legítimas

et émigrer en quelque sorte clandestinement

und gewissermaßen im Verborgenen

e inmigrar de alguna manera clandestina

furtively setting foot

---

sur les terres européennes.

europäischen Boden betreten.

al territorio europeo.

on European soil.

On parle de boat people dans ces cas-là pour décrire ce groupe de personnes.

Diese Gruppe von Leuten wird mit dem Begriff Boat people bezeichnet.

Se habla de balseros para describir a ese grupo de personas.

The expression boat people is used to describe this group of people.

„El leitmotiv de la campaña electoral de el candidato de la izquierda es la bajada de los impuestos.“

« Le leitmotiv de
la campagne électorale à gauche est la baisse des impôts. »

“The leitmotiv of the leftist candidate’s election campaign is lower taxes.”

„Das Leitmotiv der Wahlkampagne des Kandidaten der Linken ist das Senken der Steuern.“

Por ejemplo.

Juste pour exemple.

Just as an example.

Nur so als Beispiel.

Eso sería un ejemplo de leitmotiv no aplicado a la música,

Ce serait un exemple pour leitmotiv ne s’appliquant pas à la musique,

That’s an example of a non-musical leitmotiv,

Das wäre ein Beispiel für Leitmotiv, das sich nicht auf die Musik bezieht,

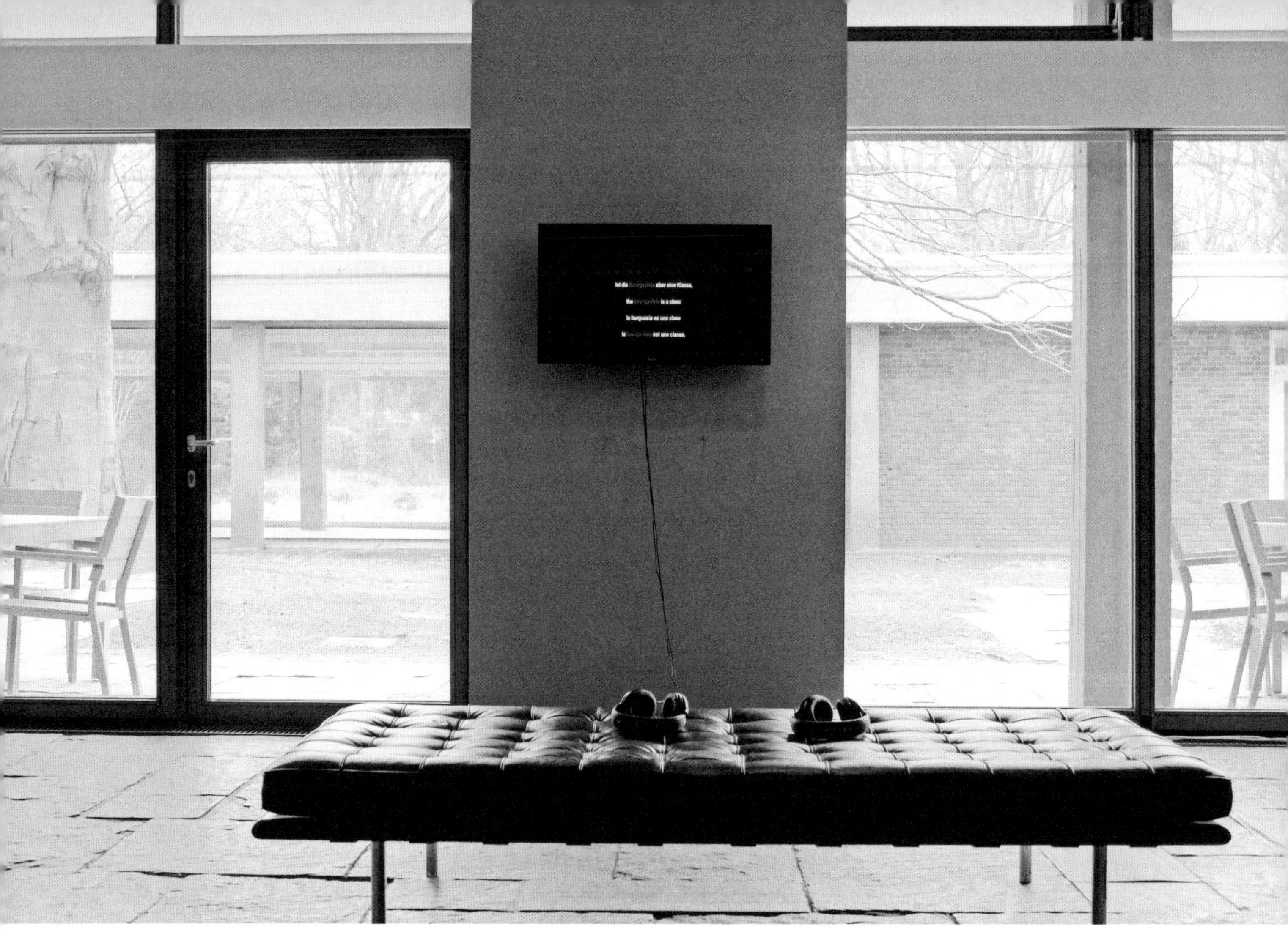

MU M

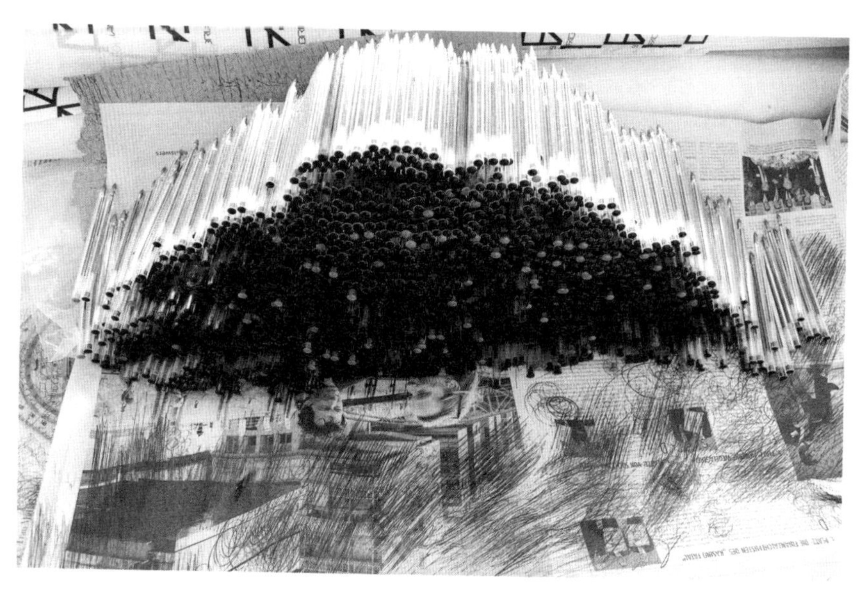

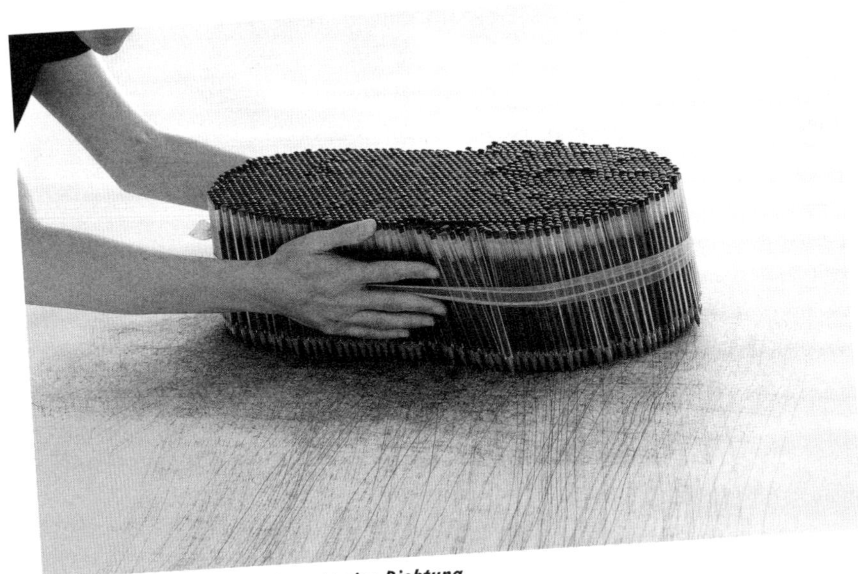

making of *Jedes Kollektiv braucht eine Richtung*

A Breath, a System

On control and loss of control in the series *Jedes Kollektiv braucht eine Richtung*

Ein Hauch, ein System

Über Kontrolle und Kontrollverlust in der Serie *Jedes Kollektiv braucht eine Richtung*

Kolja Reichert

Ich mag Kugelschreiber nicht. Ich habe nie verstanden, warum sie noch in Verwendung sind. Sie sehen hässlich aus, funktionieren selten und wenn doch, dann hinterlassen sie eine Spur ohne Spur von Impuls, Neigung oder Druck, mechanisch, gleichgültig, egal. Sie produzieren nichts außer nichtverottenden Müll. Insofern tun mir die 1805 Kugelschreiber nicht leid, die auf Nadine Fechts riesigem Ateliertisch mit Klebeband aneinander gefesselt herumstehen wie ein analoger Staubsaugerroboter. Aber mir gefallen die Bilder, die mithilfe dieses Megawerkzeugs entstehen, in ihrer kalligrafischen Leichtfüßigkeit, ihrer maschinenschreiberhaften Schwere, mit ihrem blütenstaubhaften Kontrollverlust, ihren platzenden Flecken in der reifenabriebhaften Schraffur.

Man muss sich den physischen Akt ihrer Entstehung vor Augen führen: Mit ihrer gesamten Spannweite umfasst Nadine Fecht das Trumm, hebt es an, setzt es auf das Papier auf und zwingt es erst in die eine, dann in die andere Richtung. Ruckelnd folgen die 1805 Minen, hunderte Bahnen ziehend, einige stolpern, kommen aus dem Tritt, hinterlassen auslaufende Fäden in diesem haarigen Bewegungsbild.

Keins dieser Schreibwerkzeuge ist geführt wie sonst ein Zeichenstift geführt wird, reaktionsschnell zwischen Daumen, Mittel- und Zeigefinger gelagert als äußerste Spitze einer physischen Verlängerung geistiger Konzentration, die sich ins Material übersetzt, auf die leisesten Schwingungen der Erfindungs- und Empfindungsgabe antwortend. Stattdessen sind sie aufrecht zusammengezwängt, von keiner Fingerspitze berührt, sind dumm, pressen einander gegenseitig voran, reines Gewicht, stumpfe Gewalt.

Im Kontrast dazu steht die Leichtigkeit des Ergebnisses, die sich gerade der Abwesenheit jeder Spur einer Künstlerhand verdankt: ein Hauch, ein System. Die offene Form setzt sich in der Präsentation fort, wenn das Blatt ohne Rahmen lapidar an die Wand getaped ist und in eine uneinsehbare Rolle am Boden ausläuft.

Was ist das für ein zeichnerischer Zugriff, den Nadine Fecht hier erprobt? Es ist eben nicht die Delegation des Malprozesses an Algorithmen, wie ihn Reena Spaulings (selbst ein Kollektiv) zelebrieren, wenn sie von einem Staubsaugerroboter gemalte Bilder vorstellen, was nicht mehr als ein One-Liner ist, ein Kalauer, der schnell verblasst (*Latest Landscapes*, 2017). Noch weniger hat Fechts Vorgehensweise zu tun mit Zeichenrobotern, etwa von Patrick Tresset. Und am wenigsten mit den klassischen Ideen der *écriture automatique,* die das Subjekt zugunsten eines Unbewussten zurücktreten lassen wollte. Nadine Fecht bleibt als Subjekt Herrin sowohl der groben Richtung der Linienführung als auch des Systems, das sie die Kontrolle über die einzelnen Linien verlieren lässt.

Was ist das für ein System, das Fecht dazwischenschaltet zwischen die Erfindung und das Bild? Mit dem sie den Zeichenprozess von der Schräge in die Vertikale verlegt, und vom Strich in die Fläche? Was ist die Rolle des einzelnen Schreibwerkzeugs? Auf der künstlerischen Ebene sucht Fecht im Verzicht auf zeichnerische Virtuosität nach der weitestmöglichen Zurücknahme des gestaltenden Subjekts. Auf der thematischen Ebene untersucht Fecht Kollektivierungsprozesse, die

I don't like ballpoint pens. I have never understood why they are still in use. They look ugly, rarely function and when they do they leave a trail without any trace of impulse, disposition, or pressure; mechanical, indifferent, whatever. They don't produce anything apart from non-decomposable rubbish. To this extent I am not sorry for the 1,805 ballpoint pens standing on Nadine Fecht's huge studio table, bound together with sticky tape like an analog vacuum cleaner robot. But I like the pictures created using this mega-tool, with their calligraphic light-footedness, their typist-like gravity, with their pollen-like loss of control, their exploding tire-wear-like hatching.

One has to visualize the physical act of their creation: Nadine Fecht grasps the lump in its entire width, lifts it up, places it on the paper and swings it in the one direction and then in the other. The 1,805 pen refills follow juddering, tracing hundreds of tracks, some of them stumble, lose their step, leaving threads behind which expire in the hairy pattern of movement.

None of these writing utensils are guided like a pencil is guided, with quick reactions, supported between the thumb and the middle and index finger as the outmost tip of a physical extension to intellectual concentration, which translates itself into material, responding to the slightest oscillations in the powers of invention and sensation. Instead they are forced together in the vertical position, untouched by fingertips, are dumb, pushing one another forward, pure weight, blunt force.

This stands in contrast to the result, which is precisely a consequence of the absence of all traces of the artist's hand: a breath, a system. The open form is continued in the presentation, when the sheet is casually taped to the wall without a frame, expiring in an inaccessible roll on the floor.

What is that for a graphic approach that Nadine Fecht tests here? It is not the delegation of painting processes to algorithms as celebrated by Reena Spaulings (itself a collective), when they imagine pictures painted by a vacuum cleaner robot, which is nothing more than a one-liner, a corny joke which quickly fades (*Latest Landscapes*, 2017). And Fecht's approach has even less to do with drawing robots, for example those used by Patrick Tresset. And least of all with the classic idea of *écriture automatique,* which set out to privilege an unconscious over the subject. As subject Nadine Fecht remains mistress of both the rough direction of the layout as well as the system, by means of which she is able to relinquish control over the individual lines.

What kind of system is it that Fecht inserts between the invention and the picture? With which she shifts the drawing process from the angled to the vertical, and from the line to the surface? What is the role of the individual writing utensils? On the artistic level, with her relinquishment of graphic virtuosity, Fecht searches for the fullest possible withdrawal of the subject as active shaping force. On the thematic level Fecht examines collectivization processes,

the thermodynamics of resistance (resistance of the material, resistance of the mass, resistance of the individual). One can read the ballpoint pens as parts of a collective, whose members, as soon as the totality moves in a direction, and especially then when it changes direction, either move in accord, or in some cases, break away, stumble, or become trampled underfoot. One can see the scattered red and blue lines as antagonists of the black, their tracks as a struggle for assertion.

However, this illustrative approach does not prove anything. The most decisive thing is the formal innovation that emerges here, the specific relationship between subject, material and medium: the subject reabsorbed into the meta-gesture with which the artist determines movement and its laws while factoring in a specific proportion of chance and entropy. The material of the ballpoint pens arranged into a superstructure in which the individual does not matter, but the thousands of interactions within seconds. The medium of drawing de-subjectifies and disembodies, relocating it in the systemic and fanning it out in hundreds of tracks. *There seem to be a thousand pens, and back behind those thousand pens no world.*

The resulting traces are now read contrary to their emergence: as if the hatching has fallen from the sky and has come to rest in the expanse of the white room as clouds. These clouds, created under conditions of extreme pressure, the placing of the mass on the paper, the crossing of the lines when drawing back, have an extreme aesthetic appeal. The blue and red threads woven into the black lend their structure an iridescent sense of depth.

However, these threads can neither be resolved as a picture, nor as the image of a system from which they have emerged. It is not just the subject but also the system that has covered its tracks here. The material is not the instrument of an intention, and the intention does not subordinate itself to the material. And nevertheless both are valid. It is a process with maximum openness in which the forces act against each other: no one is in control here, and at the same time no element is without influence. The lines are precipitates of the tension between material and intervention, between being-linked-together and standing-in-each-others-way, of movement and gravity, of inertia and design. They are the immediate traces of this struggle. Nadine Fecht brings to paper the maximum inherent tension of 1,805 protagonists. And this inherent tension translates into a unique, unrepeatable image. These line clouds record the conflict from which they emerged. Like a biological membrane whose perpetual transformation is frozen in a momentary image. Or like the skin of a water glass whose surface tension will break with the next drop.

Thermodynamik des Widerstands (Widerstand des Materials, Widerstand der Masse, Widerstand Einzelner). Man darf die Kugelschreiber als Teile eines Kollektivs lesen, dessen Mitglieder, sobald sich ihr Ganzes in eine Richtung bewegt, und vor allem dann, wenn es die Richtung wechselt, teils nicht mitkommen, ausreißen, stolpern, unter die Räder geraten. Man darf die eingesprengselten roten und blauen Linien als Antagonisten der schwarzen sehen, ihre Spuren als Kampf um Durchsetzung.

Aber mit diesem illustrativen Zugang ist kein Nachweis erbracht. Das Entscheidende ist die formale Neuerung, die hier entsteht, das spezifische Verhältnis von Subjekt, Material und Medium: das Subjekt zurückgenommen in die Metageste, mit der die Künstlerin Bewegung und Bewegungsgesetz bestimmt, mit den einkalkulierten Anteilen an Zufall und Entropie. Das Material der Kugelschreiber in eine Suprastruktur sortiert, in der es nicht auf den Einzelnen ankommt, sondern auf tausende Wechselwirkungen binnen Sekunden. Das Medium der Zeichnung entsubjektiviert und entleibt, ins Systemische verlegt und durch hunderte Spuren in die Breite gefächert. *Es ist, als würden tausend Stifte zeichnen, und hinter tausend Stiften keine Welt.*

Die entstehenden Spuren lesen sich nun gerade umgekehrt zu ihrer Entstehung: Als würden die Schraffuren vom Himmel fallen und in der Weite des Weißraums als Wolken zum Stehen kommen. Diese Wolken, entstanden im Moment höchsten Drucks, dem Aufsetzen der Masse aufs Papier, und durch die Kreuzung der Linien beim Zurückführen, sind von hohem ästhetischem Reiz. Die ins Schwarz gewobenen blauen und roten Fäden verleihen ihrer Struktur eine changierende Tiefenwirkung.

Diese Fäden lassen sich aber weder als Bild auflösen noch als Abbild eines Systems, aus dem sie entstanden. Nicht nur das Subjekt, auch das System hat hier seine Spuren verwischt. Weder ist das Material hier Mittel einer Absicht, noch unterwirft sich die Absicht dem Material. Und doch gilt beides. Es ist ein maximal offener Prozess, in dem die Kräfte gegeneinanderwirken: Niemand hat hier Kontrolle, und zugleich ist kein Element ohne Einfluss. Die Linien sind Niederschlagungen des Spannungsverhältnisses von Material und Eingriff, von Aneinandergekoppeltsein und Einanderimwegestehen, von Bewegung und Schwerkraft, von Trägheit und Gestaltung. Sie sind die unmittelbaren Spuren dieses Ringens. Nadine Fecht bringt das maximale Spannungspotenzial von 1805 Akteuren aufs Papier. Und dieses Spannungspotenzial übersetzt sich in ein einzigartiges, unwiederholbares Abbild. In diesen Linienwolken ist der Konflikt gespeichert, aus dem sie entstanden sind. Wie eine biologische Membran, deren fortwährende Verwandlung im Momentbild gefroren ist. Oder wie die Haut eines Wasserglases, deren Oberflächenspannung mit dem nächsten Tropfen platzen würde.

JEDES KOLLEKTIV BRAUCHT EINE RICHTUNG

 Jedes Kollektiv braucht eine Richtung **2013** **1805** Kugelschreiber auf Papier **ballpoint pens on paper** **~ 300 × 150 cm**

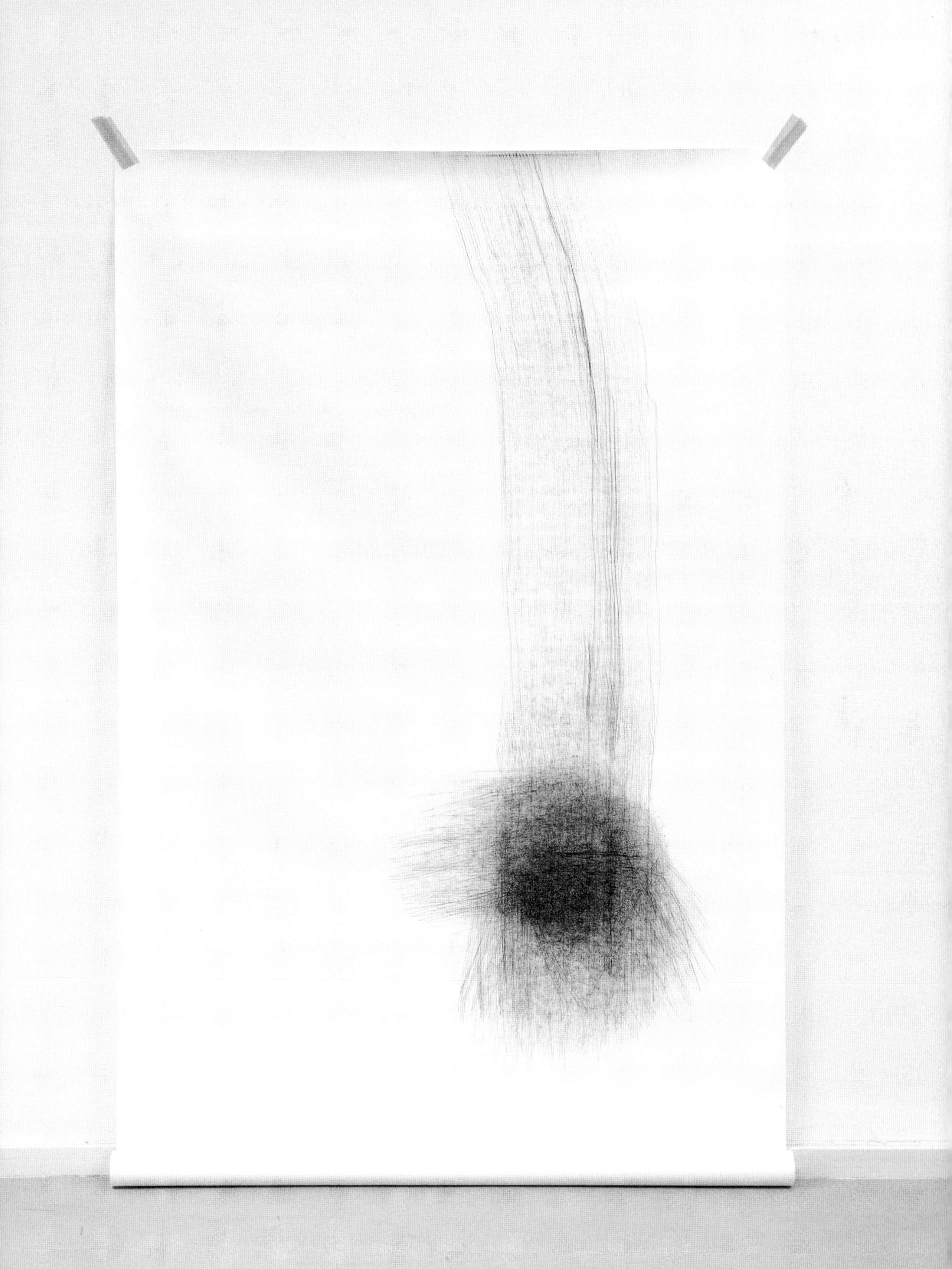

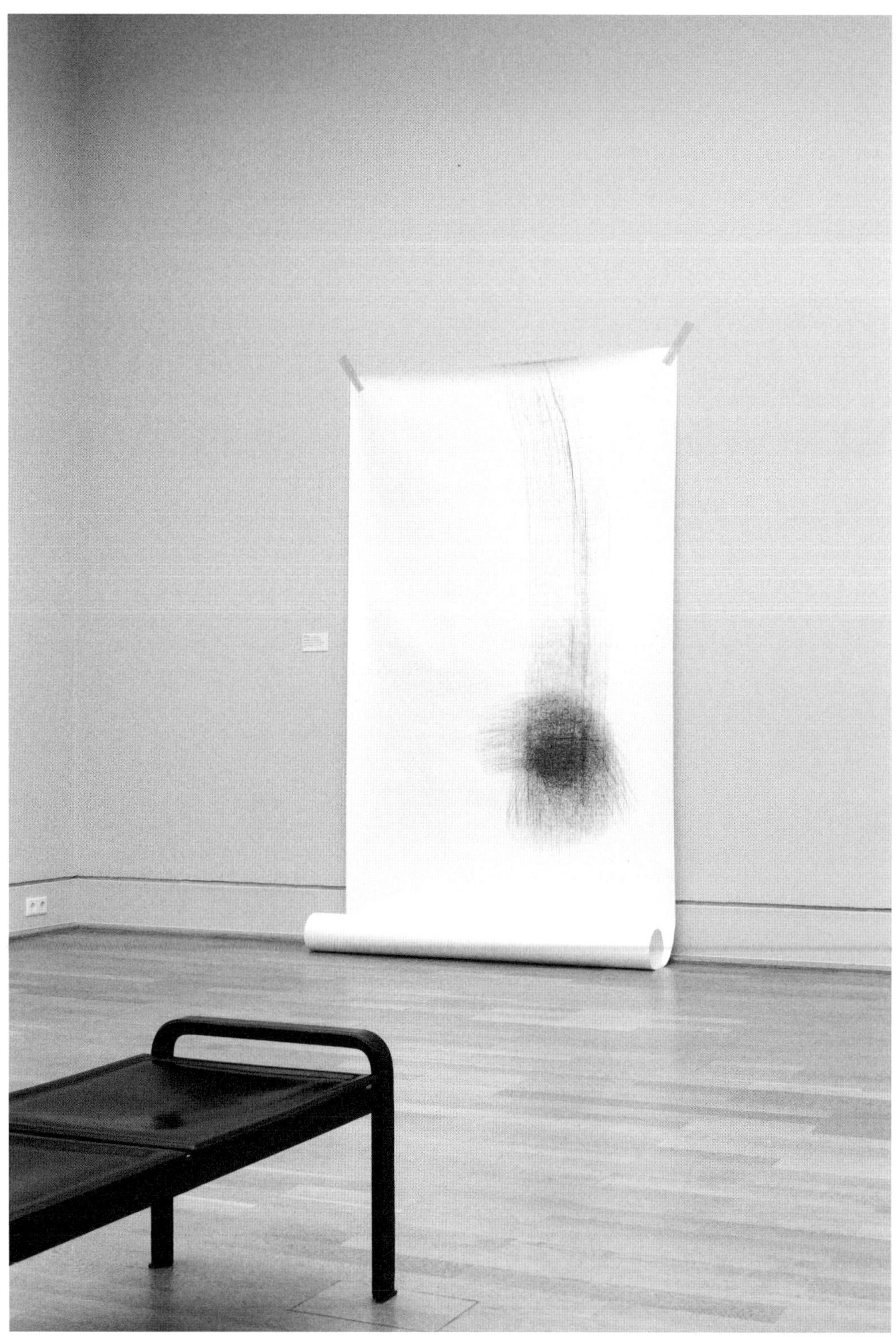

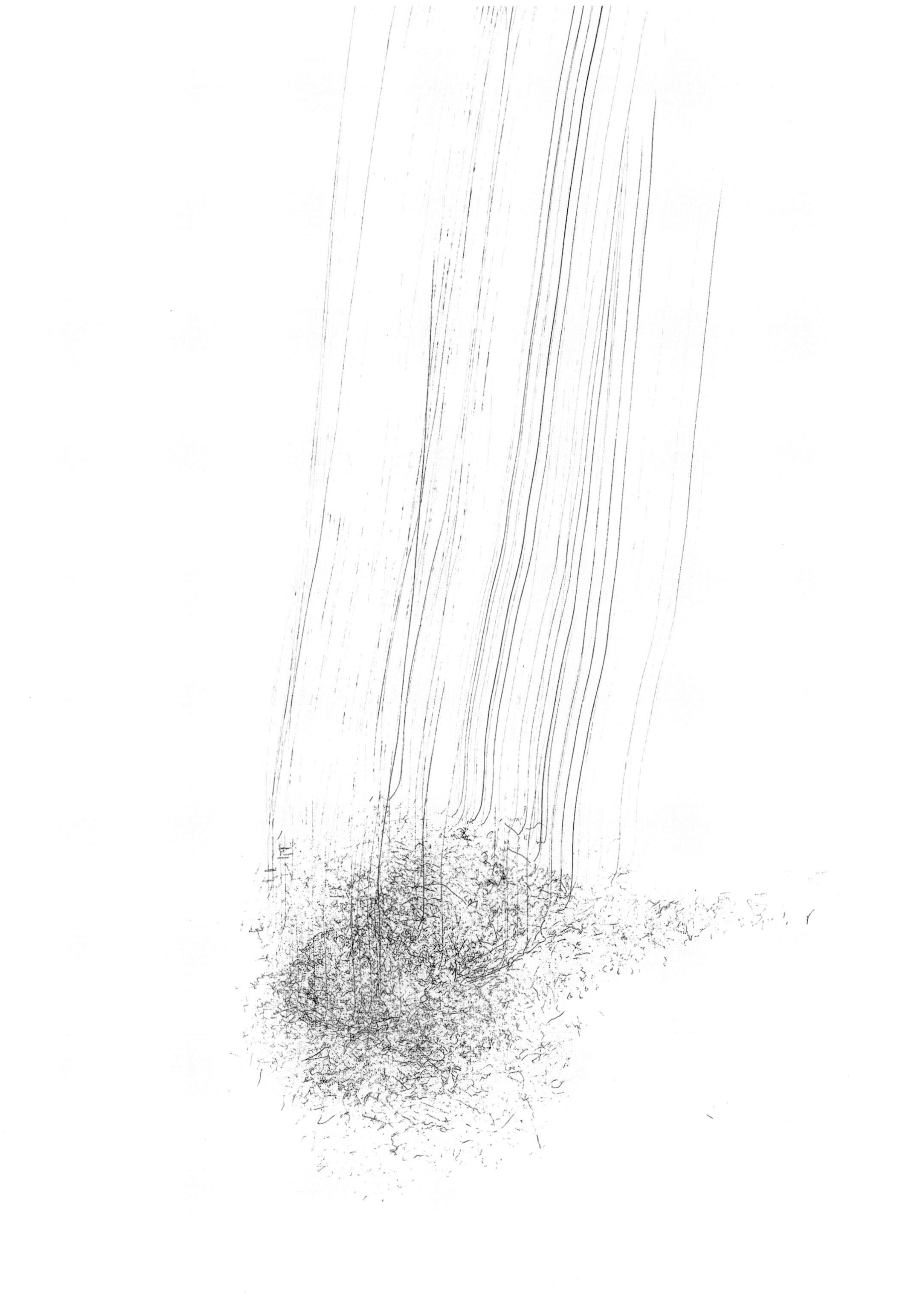

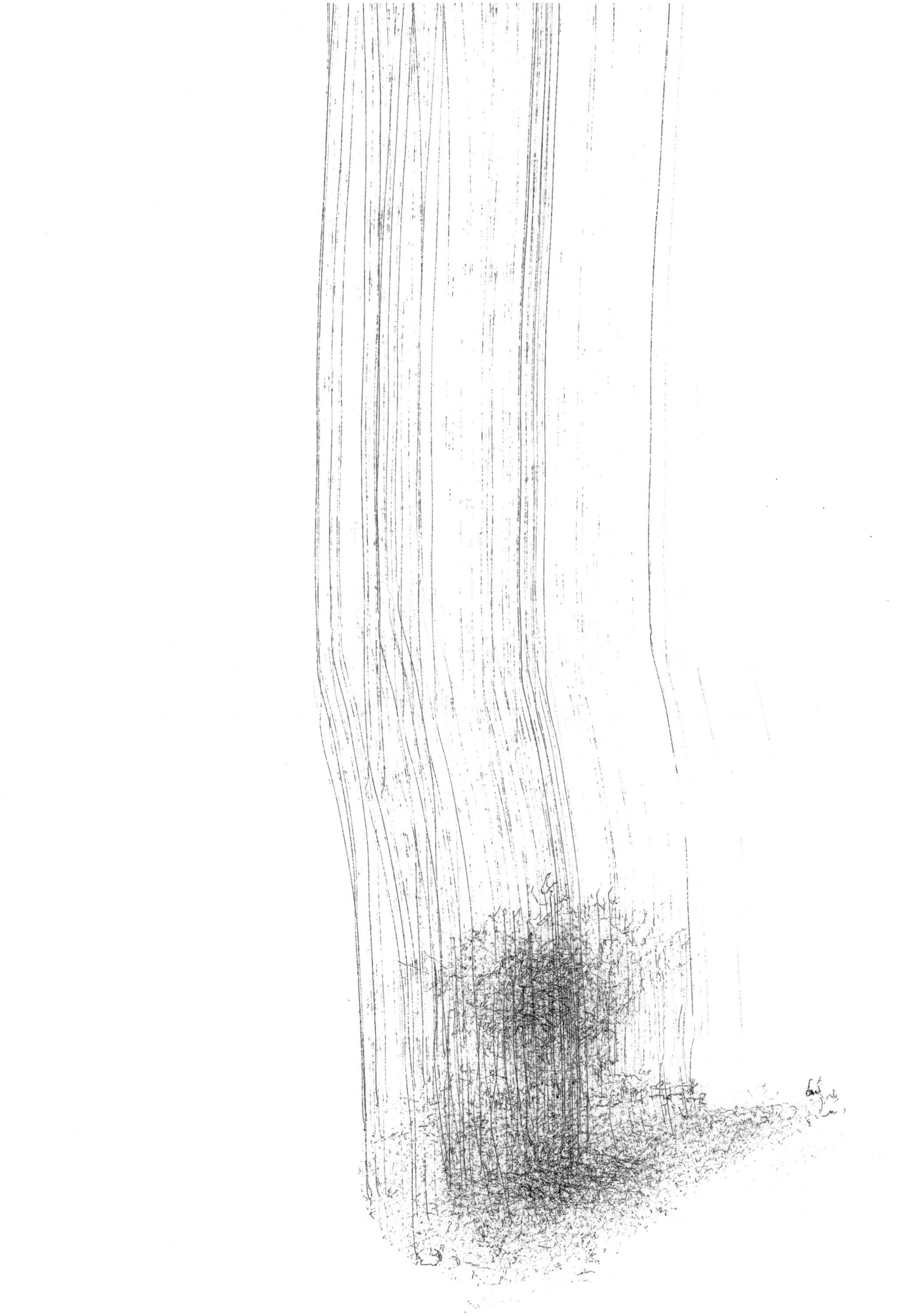

Düsz

iplim

DIE BEWEGUNG

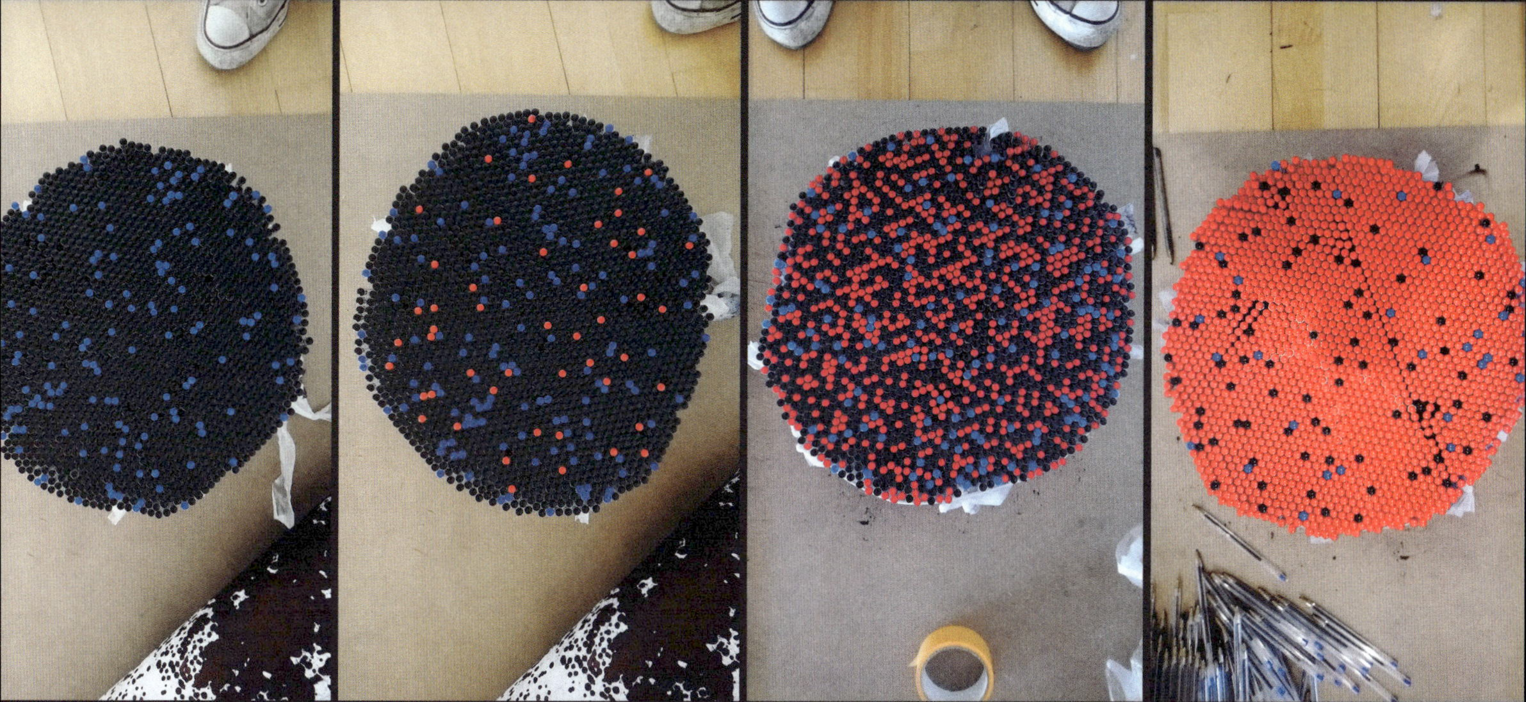

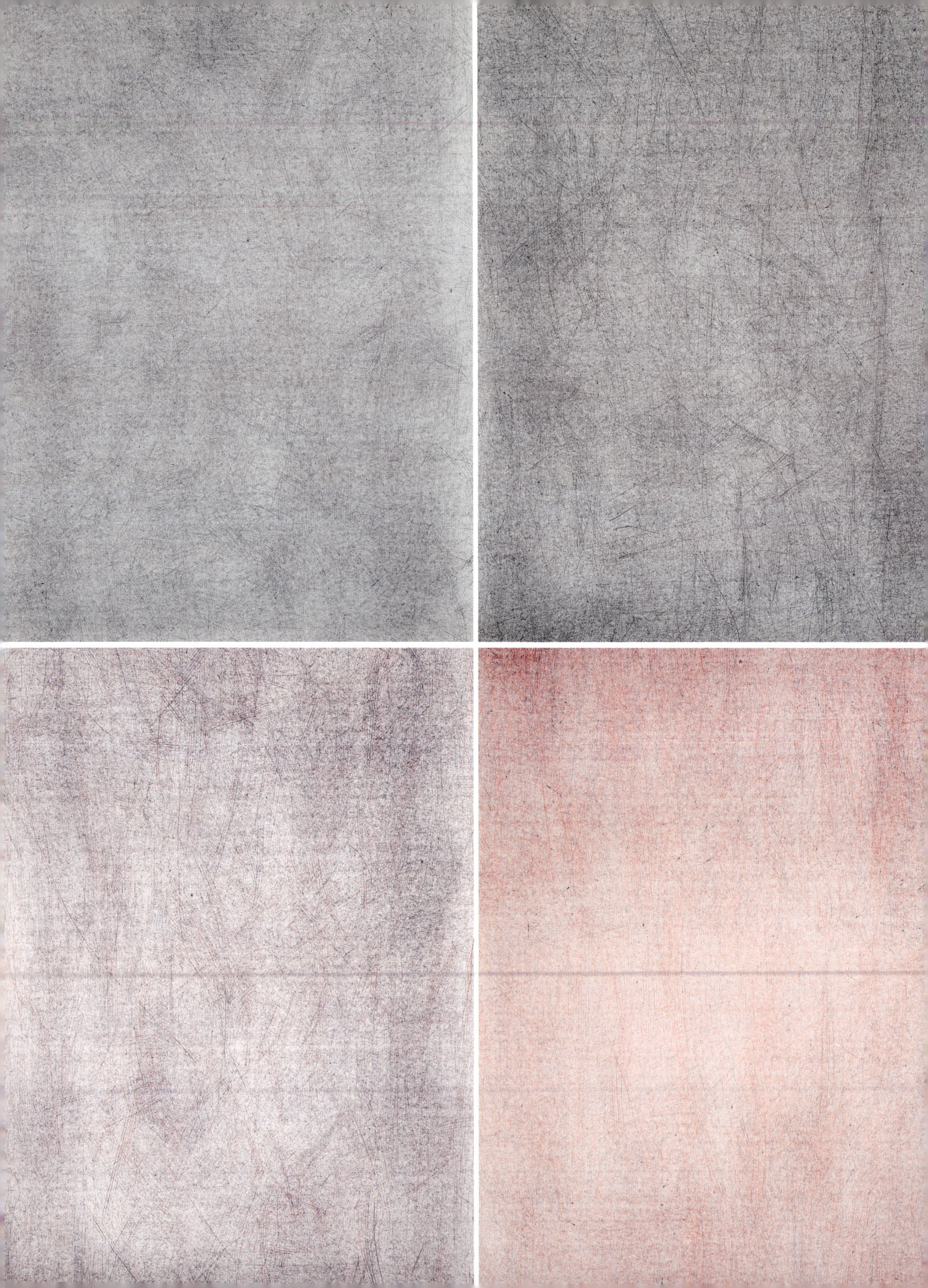

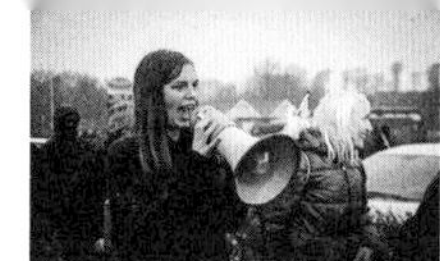

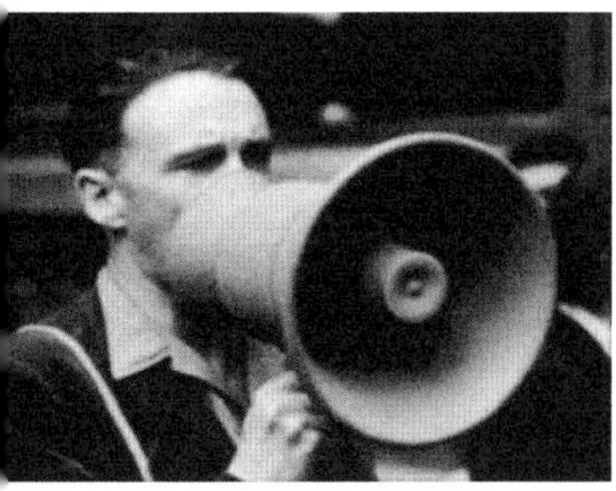

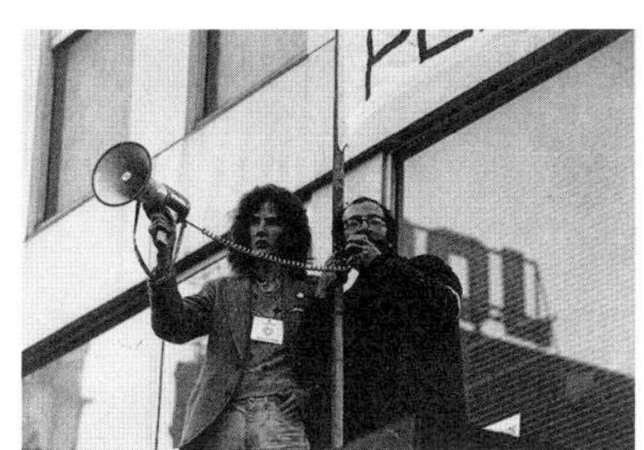

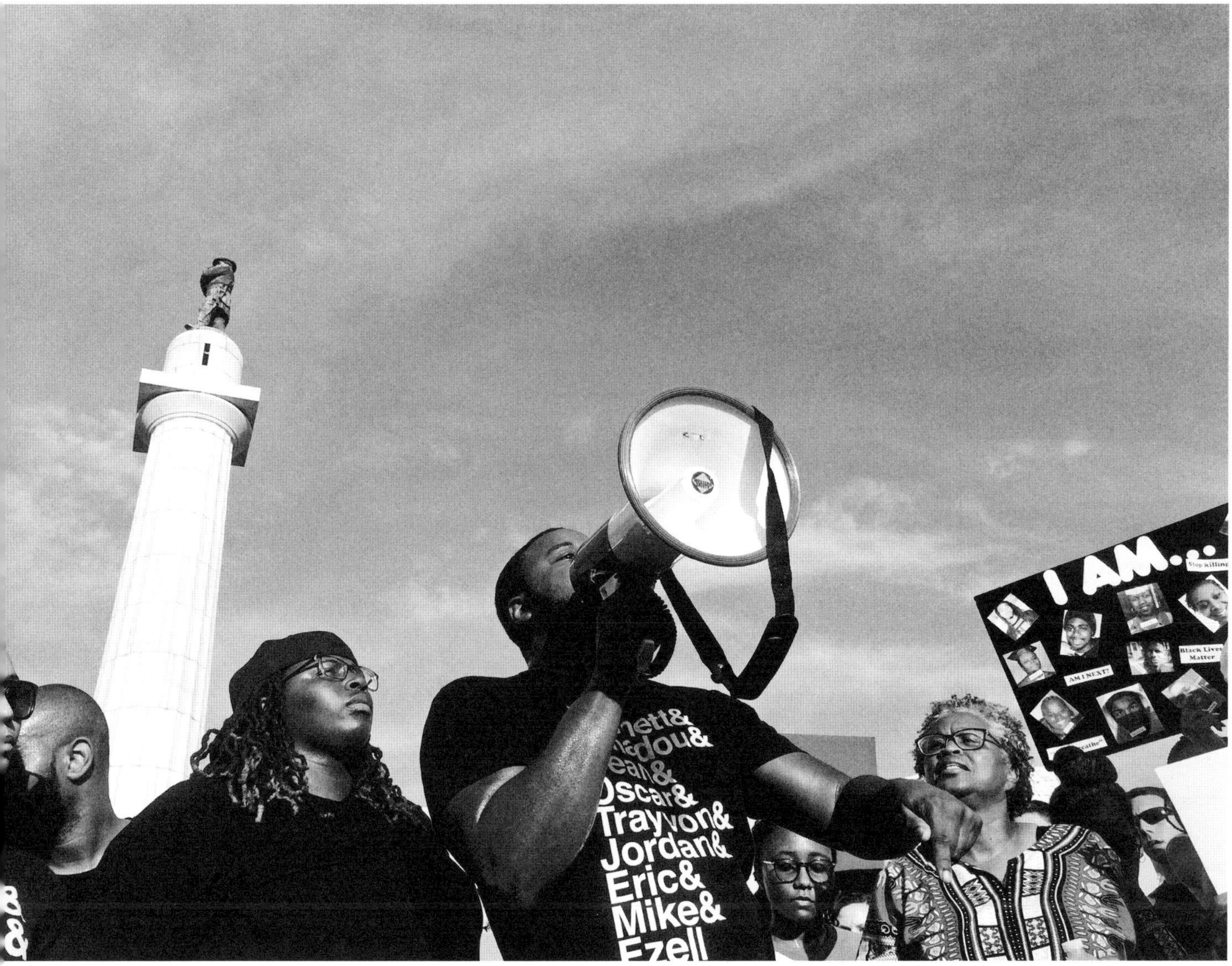

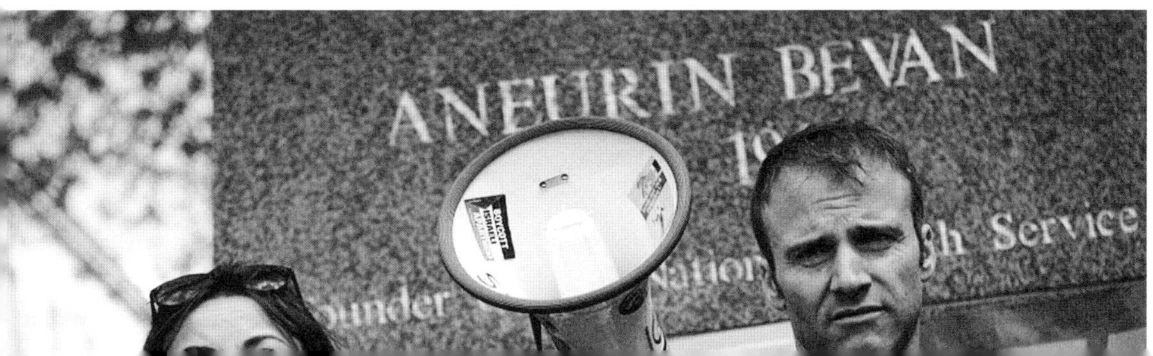
ANEURIN BEVAN

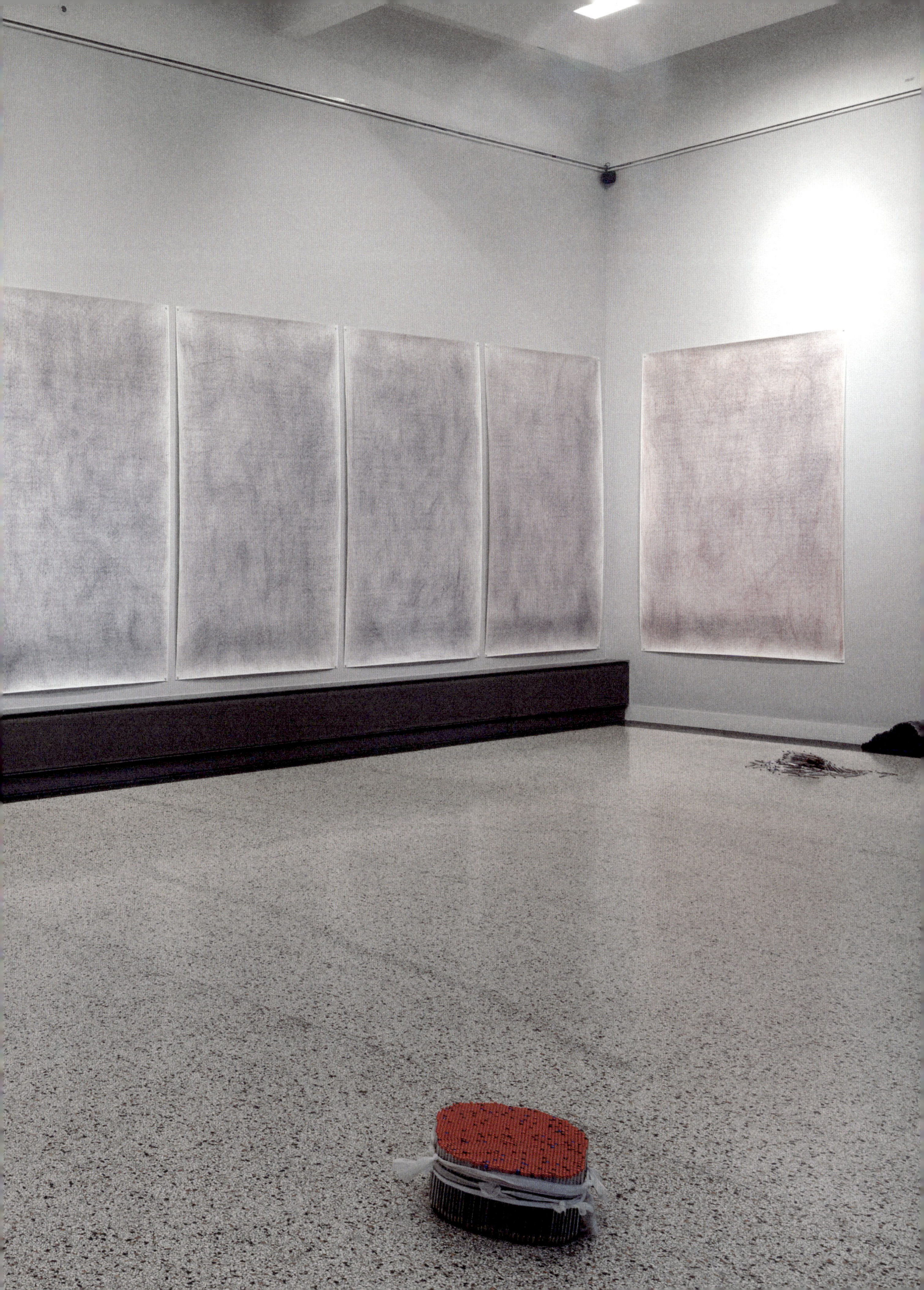

AFFIRMATION APP

Uspjet ćeš!

Možeš (ti) to!

To želiš! hoćeš

Jaka si!

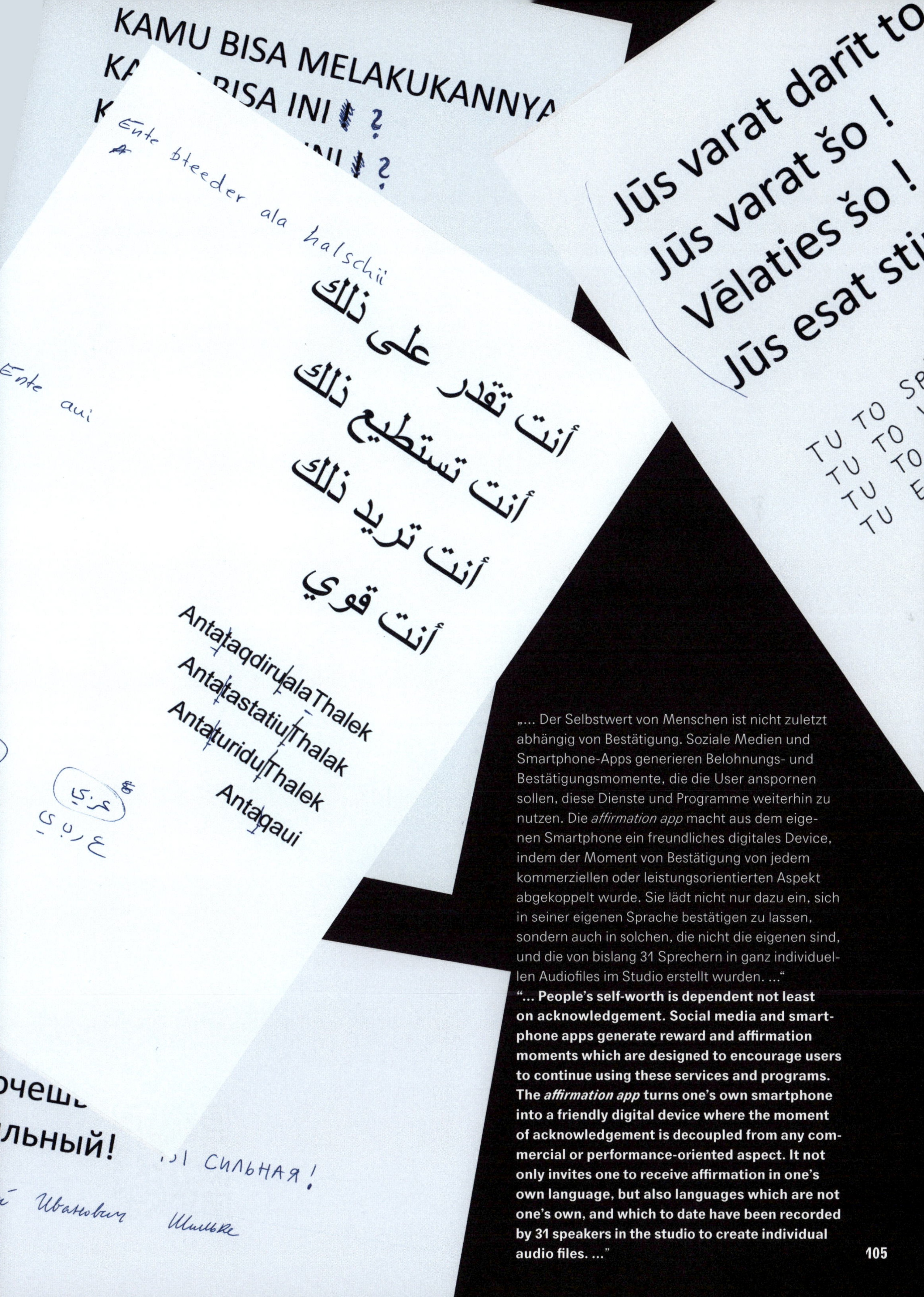

„... Der Selbstwert von Menschen ist nicht zuletzt abhängig von Bestätigung. Soziale Medien und Smartphone-Apps generieren Belohnungs- und Bestätigungsmomente, die die User anspornen sollen, diese Dienste und Programme weiterhin zu nutzen. Die *affirmation app* macht aus dem eigenen Smartphone ein freundliches digitales Device, indem der Moment von Bestätigung von jedem kommerziellen oder leistungsorientierten Aspekt abgekoppelt wurde. Sie lädt nicht nur dazu ein, sich in seiner eigenen Sprache bestätigen zu lassen, sondern auch in solchen, die nicht die eigenen sind, und die von bislang 31 Sprechern in ganz individuellen Audiofiles im Studio erstellt wurden. ...“

“... People’s self-worth is dependent not least on acknowledgement. Social media and smartphone apps generate reward and affirmation moments which are designed to encourage users to continue using these services and programs. The *affirmation app* turns one’s own smartphone into a friendly digital device where the moment of acknowledgement is decoupled from any commercial or performance-oriented aspect. It not only invites one to receive affirmation in one’s own language, but also languages which are not one’s own, and which to date have been recorded by 31 speakers in the studio to create individual audio files. ...”

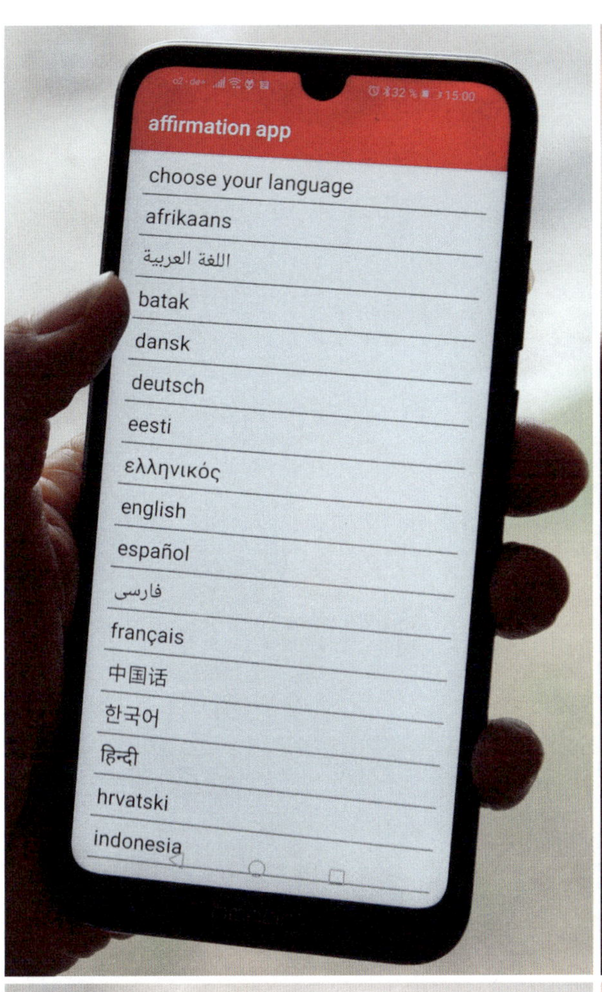
affirmation app
choose your language
afrikaans
اللغة العربية
batak
dansk
deutsch
eesti
ελληνικός
english
español
فارسی
français
中国话
한국어
हिन्दी
hrvatski
indonesia

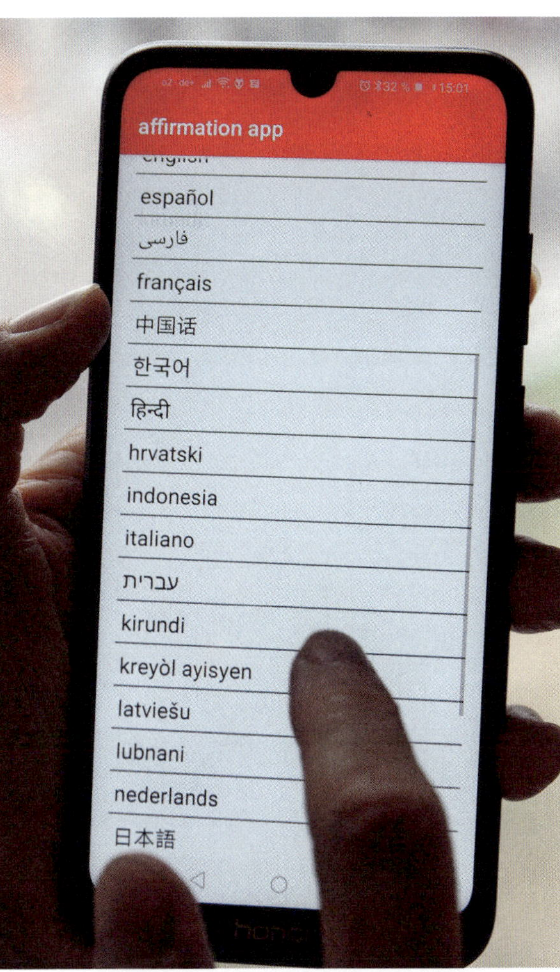
affirmation app
español
فارسی
français
中国话
한국어
हिन्दी
hrvatski
indonesia
italiano
עברית
kirundi
kreyòl ayisyen
latviešu
lubnani
nederlands
日本語

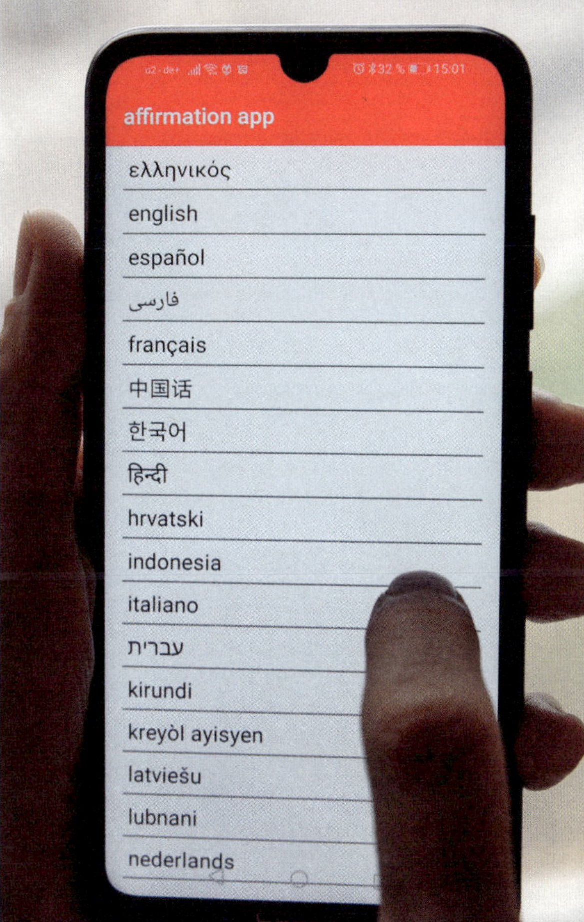
affirmation app
ελληνικός
english
español
فارسی
français
中国话
한국어
हिन्दी
hrvatski
indonesia
italiano
עברית
kirundi
kreyòl ayisyen
latviešu
lubnani
nederlands

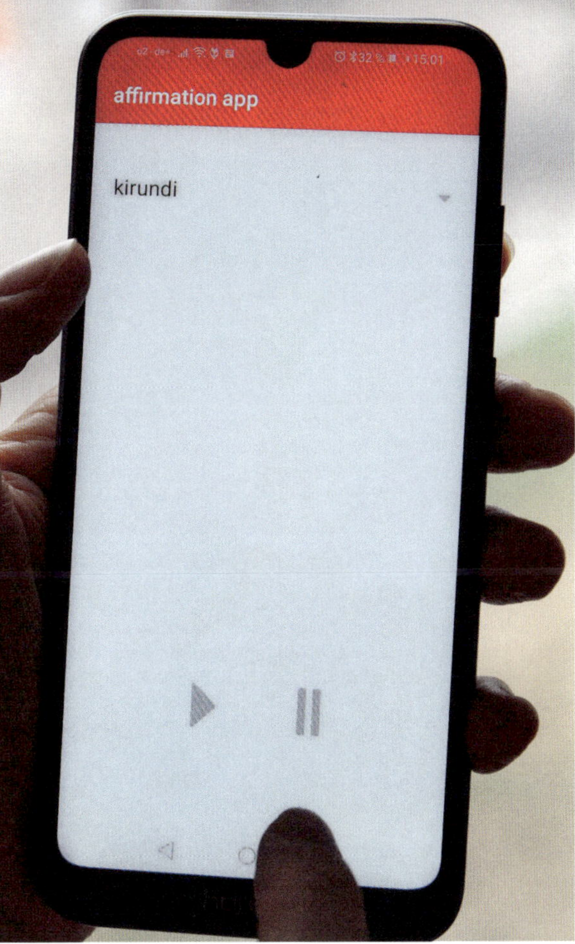
affirmation app
kirundi

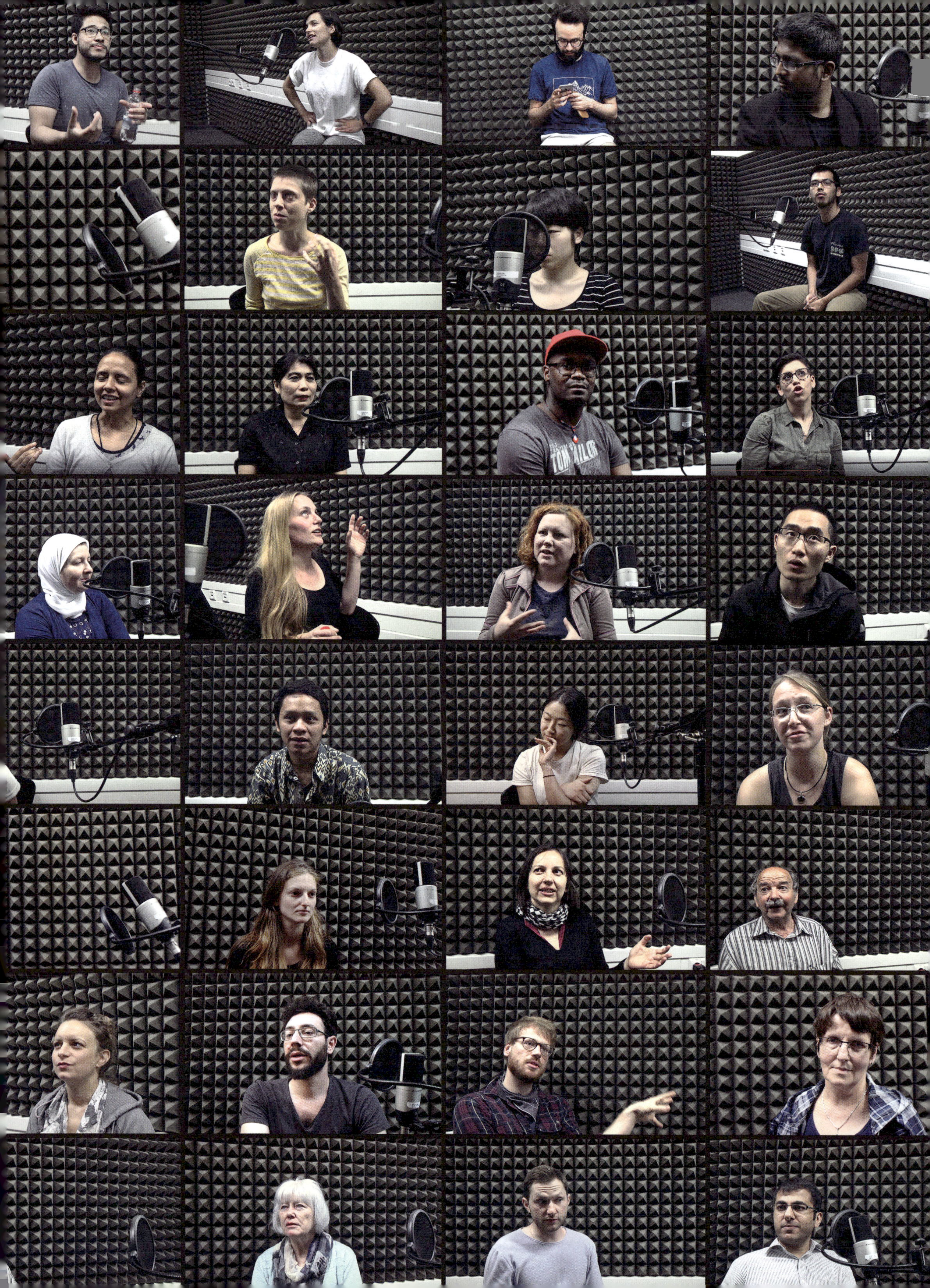

हाँ, [haa], آره [āre], yes [jɛs] – The Fragility and Openness of Being in the Work of Nadine Fecht

हाँ, [haa], آره [āre], yes [jɛs] – Die Fragilität und Offenheit des Da’Seins in Nadine Fechts Arbeiten

Krisztina Hunya

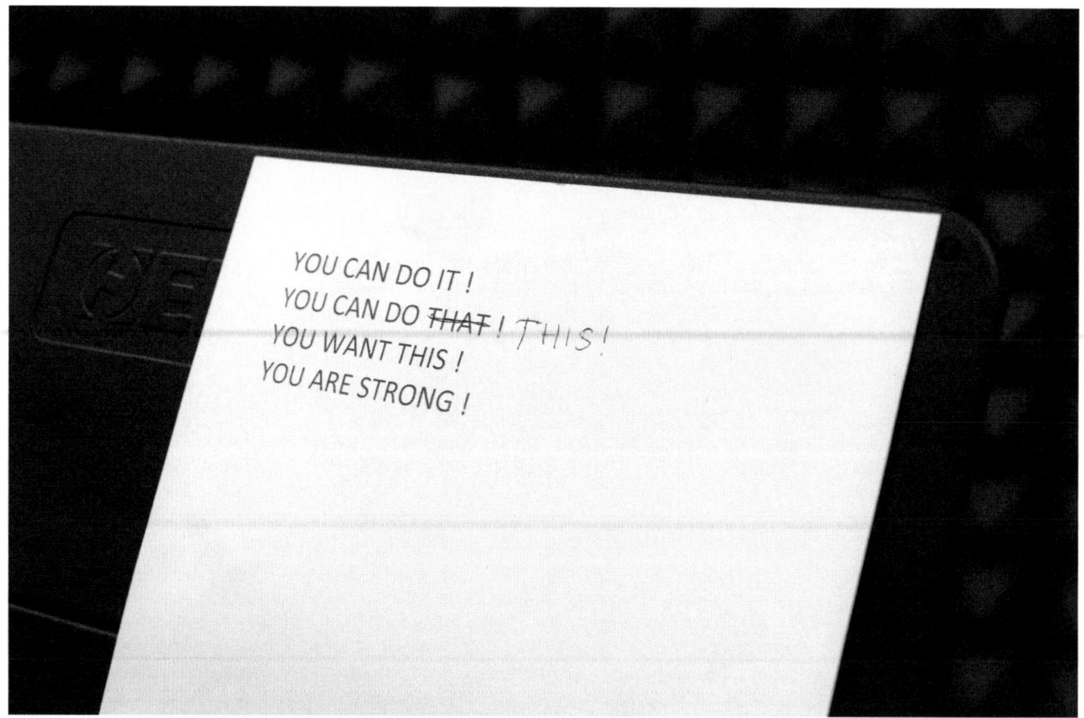

affirmation app Tonstudio Hochschule für Bildende Künste Braunschweig
recording studio Braunschweig University of Art 2016

Nadine Fecht's *affirmation app* (2017–), an Android & iOS application, which can be accessed and installed onto a smartphone using a QR code, is based on a spoken statement which can be repeated as often as desired. The phonemes, usually of one syllable in length, which to date have been captured in 31 languages, were recorded in a sound studio by native speakers. In the process the speakers respond to statements of self-assurance such as "You can do it!" or "You are strong!" with an affirmative "yes" (हाँ [haa], آره [āre], yes [jɛs], etc.). This affirmation is simultaneously addressed to oneself and the recipient; apparently it promotes self-efficacy[1]—the competence to trust oneself. At the same time the app is reminiscent of language learning programs and the promise that by repeating a series of sentences within a short space of time it is possible to master a new linguistic system.

Is it possible to train or even program self-confidence in a fluid, sometimes crisis-ridden economic environment using an app? In the context of digital utopias and dystopias, *affirmation app* raises the question of how our concept of sovereignty has been altered in times of all-encompassing technologization. Benjamin H. Bratton described this dynamic using the image of a digital mega-stack embracing the whole globe[2]—an attempt to understand the global interlinking of contemporary life with software programs, the coexistence of technological apparatuses and politico-economic decision making processes. Instead of a complex study of these interactions, Fecht resorts to the strategy of concept art: reduction, repetition, concentration.

Users of the *affirmation app* personally decide how often they want to play the response "yes" in the different languages. For example, until one hears the nuances in the Persian word हा [āre], which are hidden behind the mechanical repetition of the continuous self-affirmation.

The video work *close reading* (2013) tracks down a similar phenomenon, the cross-lingual interferences of neologisms, which often anchor aspects of global cohabitation in the respective linguistic usage. Terms such as *burnout, Angst* or *clash* describe culturally and economically determined emotional states, decisive for the challenges of a thoroughly digitalized service society. Fecht uses words and symbols at various levels: they are simultaneously material and form, and furthermore, represent the stage upon which social tensions between expectation, disappointment, and experience are played out.

At times she selects motifs of monetary value as the starting point for new experiments. The black-and-white film *sweatshop* (2015) shows a sequence of exercises, in which the surface of a dollar bill is covered with white ink. Despite the conscious absence of sound, the work produces a multisensory effect that conveys a sustained sense of exertion. The

1 The self-efficacy expectation (SEE) was developed in the 1970s by the psychologist Albert Bandura. It promises to produce greater performance by means of greater trust in one's own ability to act.

2 Benjamin H. Bratton: The Stack – On Software and Sovereignty (Software Studies), The MIT Press, Cambridge/London 2015.

Nadine Fechts *affirmation app* (seit 2017), eine Android- & iOS-Applikation, die sich über einen QR-Code finden und auf dem Smartphone installieren lässt, basiert auf einer sich beliebig oft wiederholenden, gesprochenen Bestätigung. Die bis dato in 31 Sprachen erfassten, meist einsilbigen Laute ließ Fecht von Muttersprachler_innen in einem Tonstudio aufzeichnen. Dabei reagieren die Sprecher_innen auf Sätze der Selbstversicherung wie „Du schaffst das!" oder „Du bist stark!" mit einem affirmativen „ja" (हाँ [haa], آره [āre], yes [jɛs], usw.). Diese Bestätigung ist dem Selbst und gleichzeitig dem Rezipienten zugewandt; scheinbar fördert sie die Selbstwirksamkeit[1] – die Kompetenz, sich selbst zu vertrauen. Gleichzeitig erinnert die App an Sprachlernprogramme und das Versprechen, über das Wiederholen fremdsprachlicher Satzfolgen in nur kürzester Zeit ein neues linguistisches System zu beherrschen.

Ist es möglich, das Selbstbewusstsein in einem fluiden, mitunter kriselnden ökonomischen Umfeld über eine Applikation zu trainieren, gar einzuprogrammieren? Im Kontext digitaler Utopien und Dystopien stellt *affirmation app* die Frage nach dem veränderten Konzept der Souveränität in Zeiten allumfassender Technisierung. Benjamin H. Bratton zeichnete diese Dynamik am Bild eines weltumspannenden, digitalen Megastapels *(stacks)* nach – ein Versuch, sich die globale Verflechtung des zeitgenössischen Lebens mit Softwareprogrammen, der Koexistenz technologischer Apparate und politisch-ökonomischer Entscheidungsabläufe zu vergegenwärtigen.[2] Anstelle einer komplexen Studie der Überlagerungen greift Fecht zu den Strategien der Konzeptkunst: Reduktion, Repetition, Konzentration.

Benutzer_innen der *affirmation app* entscheiden individuell wie oft sie das „Ja" auf den verschiedenen Sprachen abrufen möchten, bis man beispielsweise aus dem persischen Begriff آره [āre] die Nuancen heraushört, die sich hinter der mechanischen Wiederholung der Selbstbestätigung verbergen.

Die Videoarbeit *close reading* (2013) spürt einem ähnlichen Phänomen nach, den interlingualen Interferenzen von Neologismen, die oft Aspekte des globalen Zusammenlebens im jeweiligen Sprachgebrauch verankern. Begriffe wie *burnout, Angst* oder *clash* beschreiben kulturell und ökonomisch bedingte Gefühlszustände, ausschlaggebend für die Herausforderungen einer durchweg digitalisierten Dienstleistungsgesellschaft. Fecht nutzt Worte und Zeichen auf mehreren Ebenen: Sie sind Material und Form zugleich und stellen darüber hinaus den Austragungsort, auf dem soziale Spannungen zwischen Erwartung, Enttäuschung und Erfahrung präsent werden.

Mitunter wählt sie Motive der monetären Wertigkeit als Ausgangspunkt neuer Versuchsanordnungen. Der Schwarzweißfilm *sweatshop* (2015) zeigt eine Folge von „Schwitz-Übungen", in denen die Oberfläche eines Dollarscheins mit weißer Tusche bedeckt wird. Trotz des bewussten Verzichts auf Ton ist der Arbeit eine multisensorische Wirkung eigen, die eine konstante

1 Die Selbstwirksamkeitserwartung (SWE) wurde in den 1970er-Jahren von dem Psychologen Albert Bandura entwickelt. Sie verspricht aufgrund eines höheren Vertrauens in die eigene Handlungssicherheit auch ein höheres Leistungsvermögen.

2 Benjamin H. Bratton: The Stack – On Software and Sovereignty (Software Studies), The MIT Press, Cambridge / London 2015.

Also, Burnout heißt: ein Zustand totaler Erschöpfung,

Entonces, burnout significa: Un estado de fatiga completa,

Burnout is a state of complete exhaustion.

Donc burnout signifie : un état d'épuisement complet,

close reading **00:26:52**

Anstrengung transportiert. Die weißen Linien überlagern die Banknote und treten gegeneinander an: Die erste Schicht verbirgt, die nächste enttarnt das Trägermotiv bis eine dichte Schraffur den Geldschein vollständig überlagert. Programmatisch wird Fechts Auseinandersetzung mit Konzepten von Werthaftigkeit in der wandfüllenden Arbeit *surplus* (2013/18). Über Jahre gesammelt und akribisch als Raster installiert, fügen sich Billigwaren-Preisschilder zu einer symbolischen Raum-Zeit-Achse, auf der die Indifferenz des Warenflusses und die Herausforderung ihrer ständigen Bewältigung zum Ausdruck kommen. Für Fecht steht jedes Preisschild sinnbildlich für ein Individuum mit Eigenwert, dem über die netzwerkartige Logik des Marktes ein individueller Tauschwert zusteht. Der titelgebende Mehrwert *(surplus)* verweist hier auf den Überschuss, die offene Möglichkeit, die sich abseits der Marktmechanismen ergibt und sich dadurch konventionellen Wertzumessungen entzieht.

Eine ähnlich unscheinbare Potenzialität schwingt im Auftaktgeräusch mit, das anklingt, wenn die Nadel des Plattenspielers das Vinylblatt berührt, und wird somit zum Ausgangspunkt des Werks *53 beginnings* (2012). Das Kratzen, Knistern, Pochen und Rauschen 53 verschiedener Einlaufrillen verbindet sich auf Fechts Schallplattenarbeit zu einer Abfolge spannungsvoller Momente der Erwartung (noch-nicht-hören) und Nuancierung (immer-anders-hören). Statt eine klanglich-sprachlich interpretierbare Partitur zu spielen, stellt *53 beginnings* den Akt des Zuhörens und Aufmerksam-Werdens selbst zur Disposition – eine Reminiszenz an Alvin Luciers minimalistisches Tonbandmeisterwerk *I Am Sitting in a Room* (1969). Fechts Werk entfaltet sich als synästhetische Erfahrung, als geräuschvolle Zeichnung und haptische Lautfolge.

white lines are superimposed on the banknote and compete with each other: the first layer hides while the next layer uncovers the underlying motif until a thick hatching completely covers the dollar bill. Fecht's engagement with concepts of value is given programmatic form in the wall-sized work *surplus* (2013/18). Collected over several years, and meticulously assembled to form a grid, price labels from cheap goods combine to form a symbolic space-time axis that expresses the indifference of the flood of goods and the challenge of their continual mastery. For Fecht each price label is a metaphor for an individual with their own intrinsic worth which is assigned its own exchange value by means of the network-like logic of the market. The title *surplus* refers to an excess, the open possibility that exists beyond the mechanisms of the market and thus escapes conventional valuation.

A similar discreet potential resonates in the initial sound produced when the needle of a record player touches the vinyl disc, which forms the starting point for the work *53 beginnings* (2012). The scratching, crackling, popping, and hissing of the 53 different lead-in grooves on the phonographic work combine to form a sequence of tension-laden moments of expectation (not yet hearing) and nuance (always hearing differently). Instead of playing a score which can be interpreted audio-linguistically, *53 beginnings* explores the act of hearing and becoming attentive—reminiscent of Alvin Lucier's minimalist audio tape masterpiece *I Am Sitting in a Room* (1969). Fecht's work unfolds as a synesthetic experience, as a noise-filled drawing and a haptic phonetic sequence.

It is not the indifference with which we encounter the ubiquitous expressions and price labels, the crackling and the lines, which makes them special for the artistic engagement. It is the fact that they combine an openness, a potential which can be perceived through a conscious positioning and sensitisation. While Fecht uses these to awaken new layers of perception and to question their modes of existence, openness is also a concept from management theory, which although it deviates from the artistic intention, still enriches the work with a further layer of associations. Theories dedicated to organizational efficiency and productivity promote open structures, "flexible" processes and conditions, especially in the post-industrial age. Guillaume Paoli has identified the desire to "make human material pliant" in this demand for flexibility,[3] management's dream of creating people—producers and consumers—whose being is like capital itself: industrious and egoistic. In late capitalist societies this demand also has a qualitative nature, even the call centre employee—the contemporary representative of the production line worker—should respond to individual demands with self-confidence and endurance, smiling into the telephone: हा [haa], آره [āre], yes [jɛs]. Fecht's oeuvre reveals the tensions and ambivalences between intrinsic value and worthlessness, the value of goods and the value of work, through to a person's value, in order to emphasize the intangibility and fragility of "being here, existing, as a human being, in a basically uncertain and insecure position in the world".[4]

3 Guillaume Paoli, Technik der Zombifikation, in: Reinigungsgesellschaft and Miklós Erhardt: The Social Engine – Exploring Flexibility, SoYAA – Galerie ACC, Budapest/Weimar 2007, p. 105.

4 Jürgen Dehm: Interview – Nadine Fecht, artfridge.de, August 28, 2014, http://www.artfridge.de/2014/08/interview-nadine-fecht.html, (Status: June 16, 2019).

Es ist nicht die Indifferenz, mit der wir den ubiquitären Redewendungen und Preisschildern, dem Knistern und den Linien begegnen, die sie für die künstlerische Auseinandersetzung besonders machen. Sie verbindet die Offenheit, eine Potenzialität, die durch eine bewusste Positionierung und Sensibilisierung wahrgenommen werden kann. Während Fecht diese nutzt, um neue Wahrnehmungsebenen wachzurufen und ihre Existenzmodi zu befragen, ist Offenheit auch ein Konzept der Managementtheorie, das zwar konzeptuell von der künstlerischen Absicht abweist, aber die Assoziationsebenen des Werks um eine weitere bereichert. Theorien, die sich der organisatorischen Effizienz und Produktivität verpflichten, fördern insbesondere im postindustriellen Zeitalter offene Strukturen, „flexible" Prozesse und Zustände. Guillaume Paoli hat in dieser Forderung nach Flexibilität „das Biegsamwerden des Menschenmaterials"[3] erkannt, in der sich die Hoffnung des Managements widerspiegelt, einen Menschen – Produzenten und Konsumenten – zu schaffen, dessen Wesen so ist wie das Kapital: fleißig und egoistisch. In der spätkapitalistischen Gesellschaft ist diese Anforderung auch qualitativer Natur, sogar der Call-Center-Mitarbeiter_in – der zeitgenössische Vertreter des Fließbandarbeiters – soll individuellen Ansprüchen selbstbewusst und mit Ausdauer begegnen, in das Telefon lächeln: हा [haa], آره [āre], yes [jɛs]. Fechts Œuvre offenbart die Spannungen und Ambivalenzen zwischen dem Eigenwert und Unwert, dem Warenwert und Arbeitswert hin zum Wert eines Menschen, um auf die Intangibilität und Fragilität hinzuweisen, die „das ‚Da sein', existieren, als Mensch, in einer prinzipiell unsicheren und ungesicherten Stellung in der Welt"[4] nahelegt.

3 Guillaume Paoli, Technik der Zombifikation, in: Reinigungsgesellschaft und Miklós Erhardt: The Social Engine – Exploring Flexibility, SoYAA – Galerie ACC, Budapest/Weimar 2007, S. 105.

4 Jürgen Dehm: Interview – Nadine Fecht, artfridge.de, 28. August 2014, http://www.artfridge.de/2014/08/interview-nadine-fecht.html, (Stand: 16.6.2019).

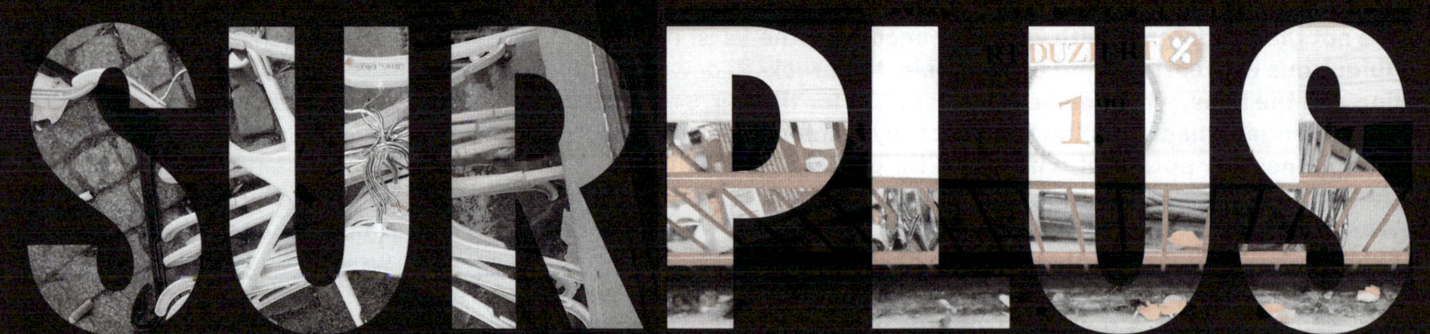

 surplus **2013/18** gefundene Preisschilder auf Wand **found price tags on wall** Maße variabel **dimensions variable**

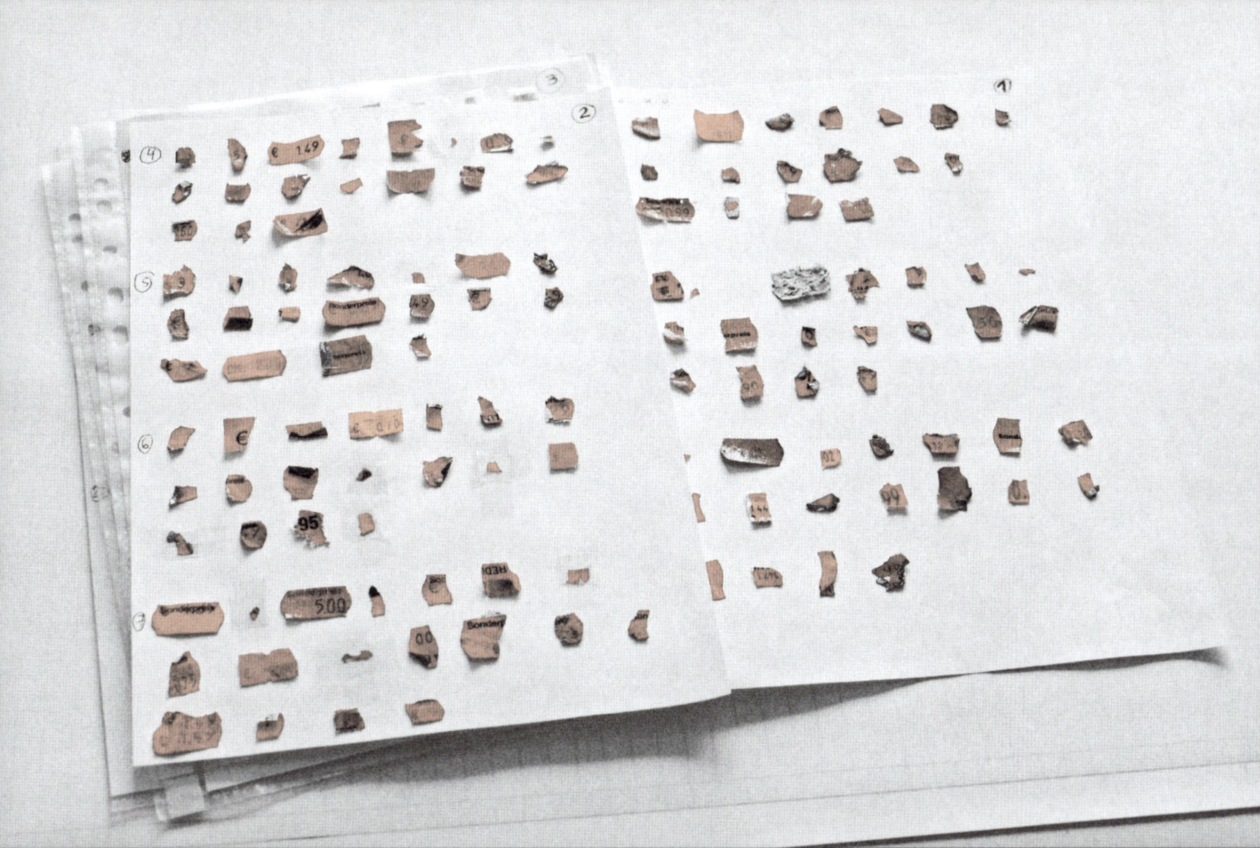

Sammlung gefundener Preisschilder **collection of found price tags**

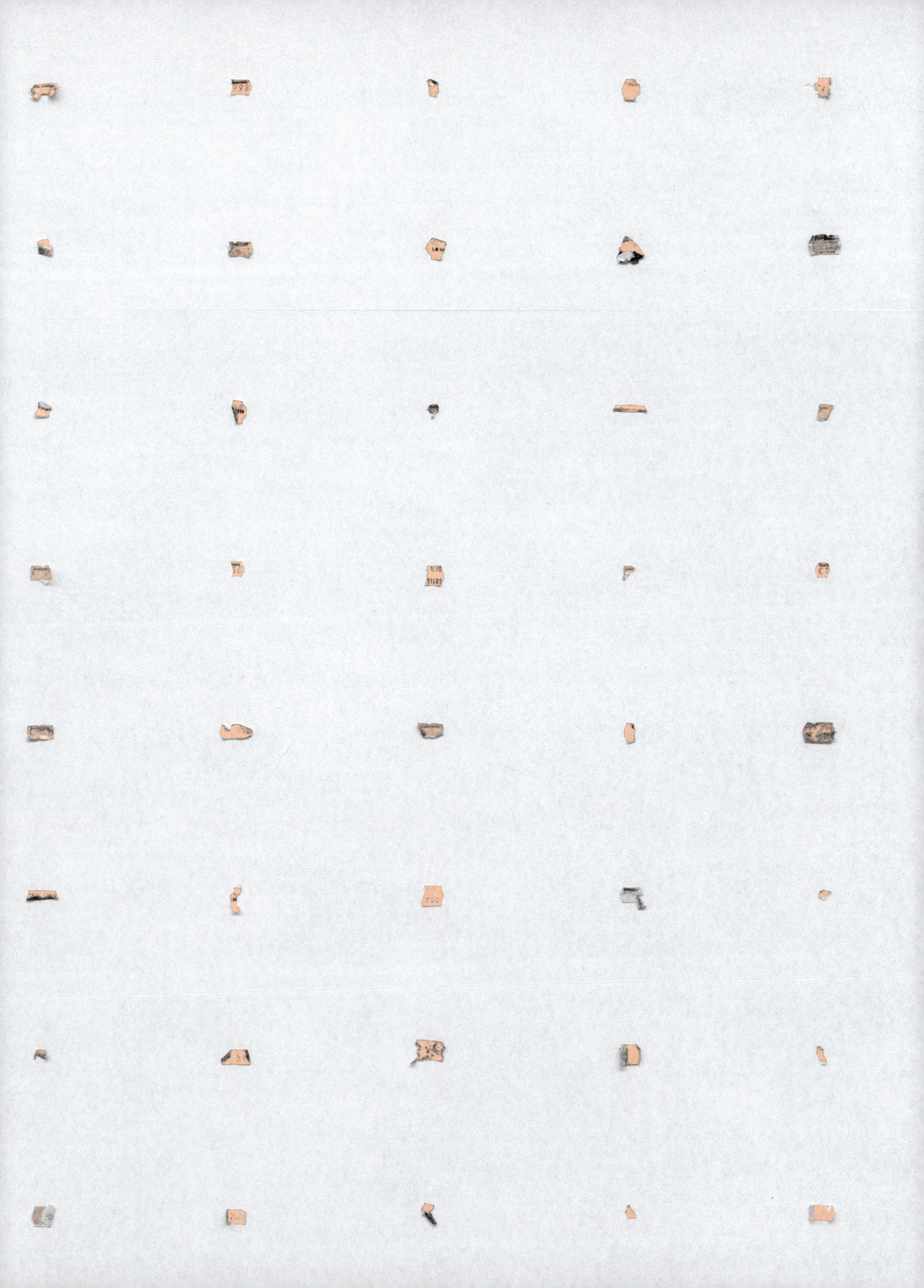

SWEATSHOP

 sweatshop 2016 HD Videoloop

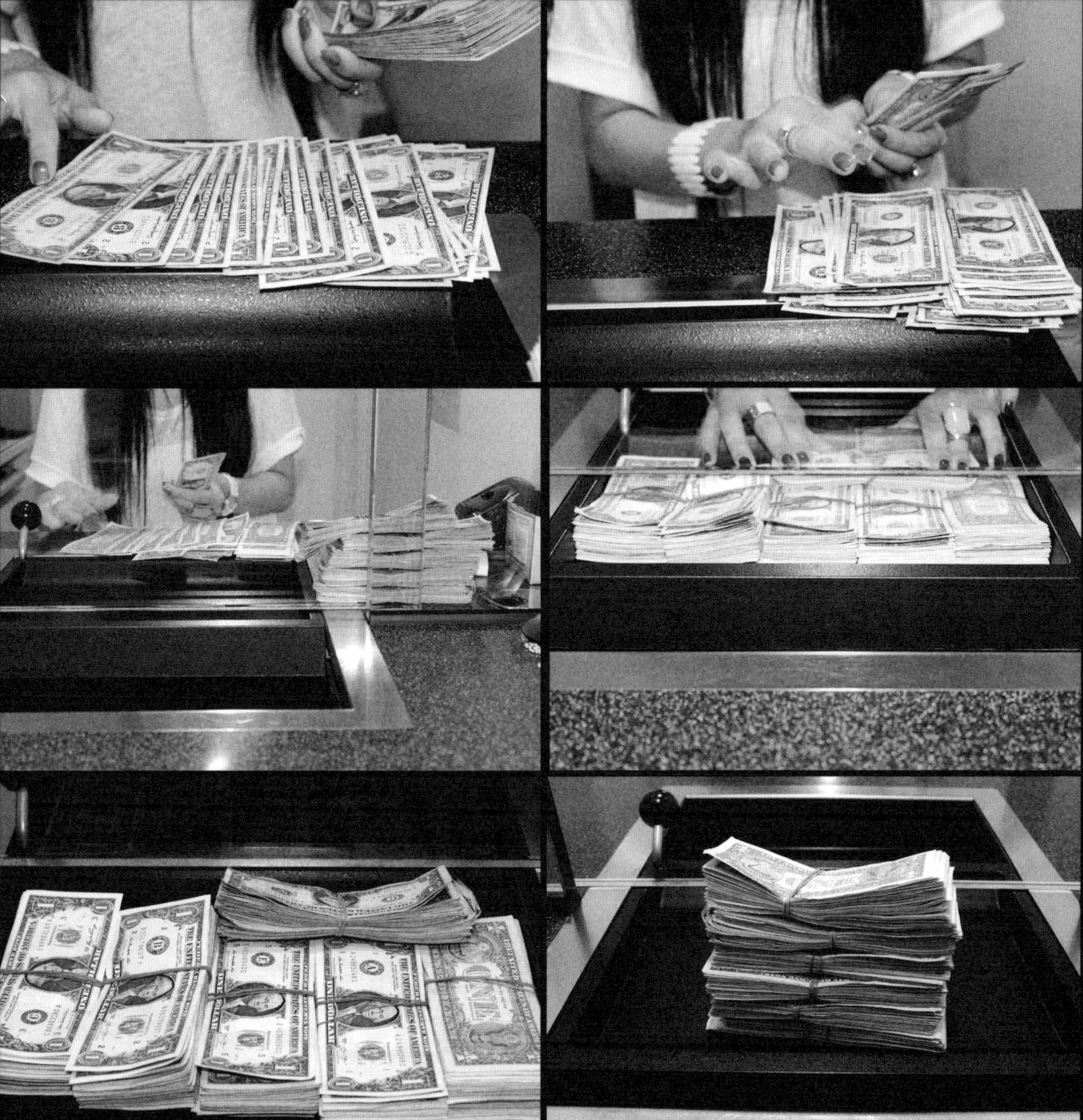

sweatshop Beschaffung der Devisen **acquisition of the currency**

„*sweatshop* zeigt als Film einen geloopten Arbeitsprozess. Arbeit als Möglichkeit der Aneignung. Arbeit aber auch als strukturelles Element von Ausbeutung. Dass für mich Kunst prinzipiell nicht von der Sphäre und den Bedingungen der Welt der Arbeit getrennt ist, ist eine zusätzliche Ebene dieses Films, der während der Erstellung der Arbeit *subjectivity as a material to trade / Subjektivität als Material zu handeln* entstanden ist."

"*sweatshop* shows a film loop of a work process. Work as the possibility of appropriation. But also work as a structural element of exploitation. That art, in my opinion, cannot on principle be separated from the sphere and conditions of the world of work is an additional level of this film which emerged during the creation of *subjectivity as a material to trade / Subjektivität als Material zu handeln*."

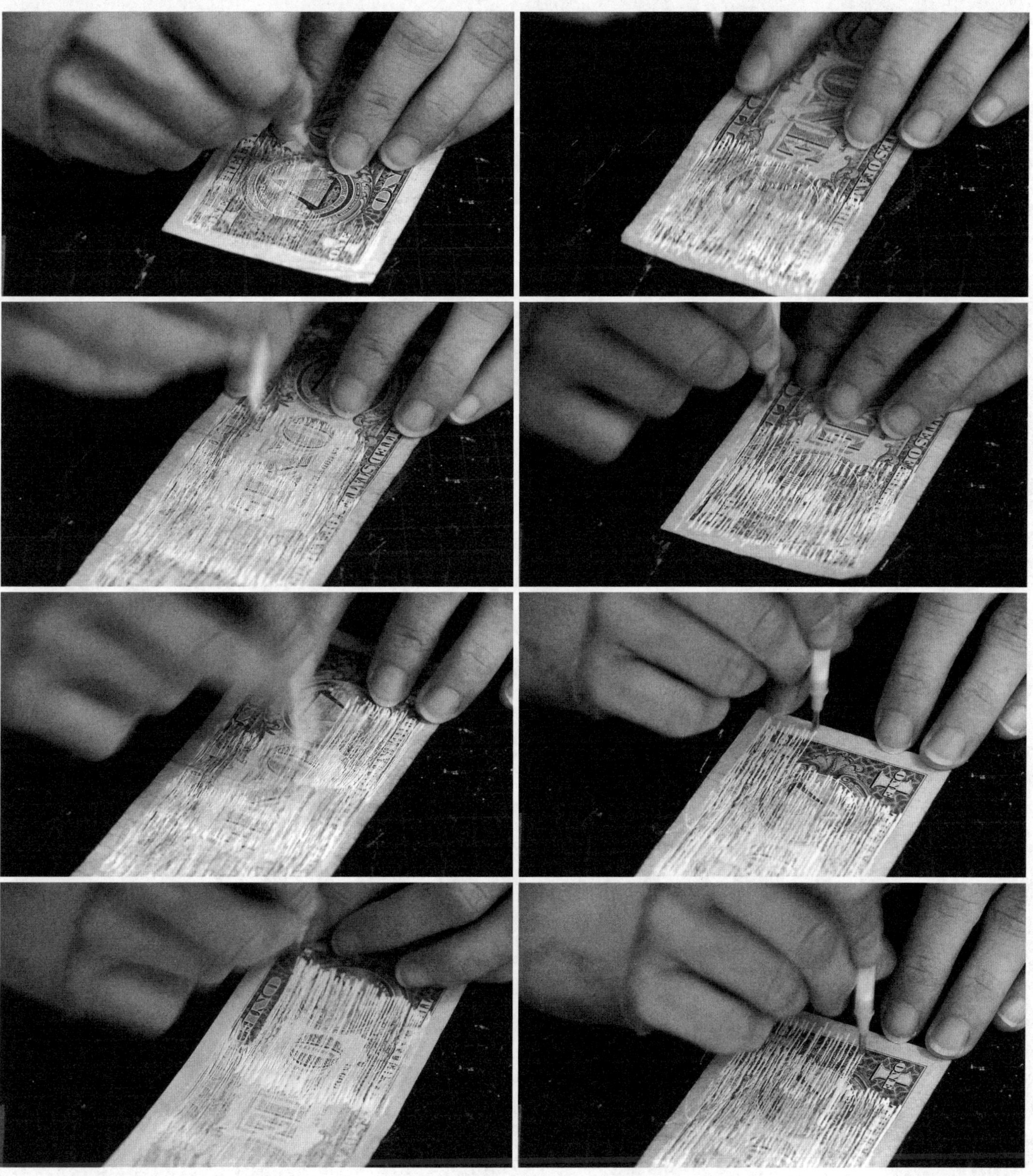

SUBJECTIVITY AS A MATERIAL TO TRADE / SUBJEKTIVITÄT ALS MATERIAL ZU HANDELN

subjectivity as a material to trade / Subjektivität als Material zu handeln 2014
weiße Tusche und transparentes Klebeband auf 960 gebrauchten 1 USD Banknoten
white ink and transparent tape on 960 used 1 USD banknotes 256 × 401 cm and neon

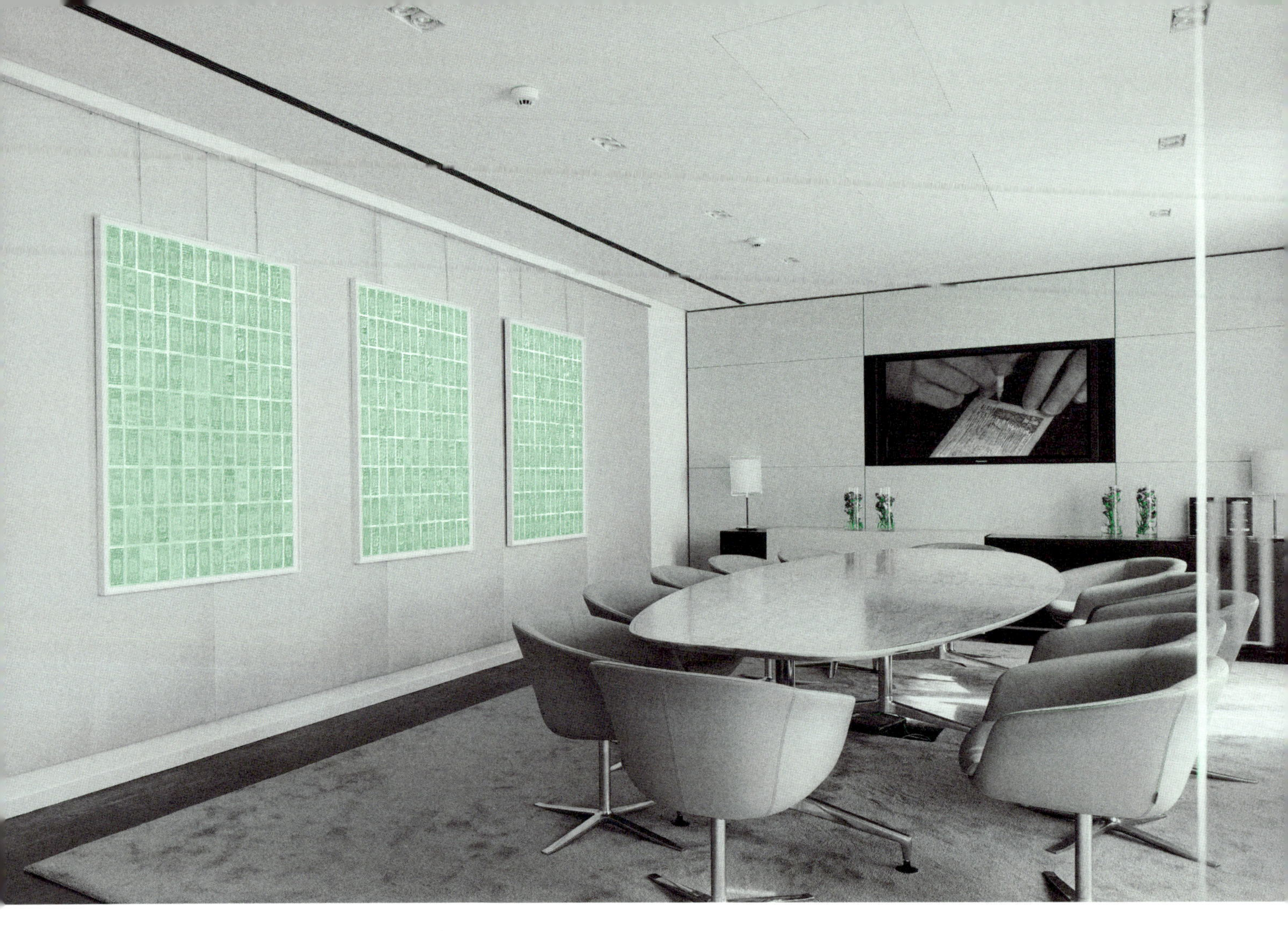

FEDERAL RESERVE NOTE
THE UNITED STATES OF AMERICA
ONE DOLLAR
ONE

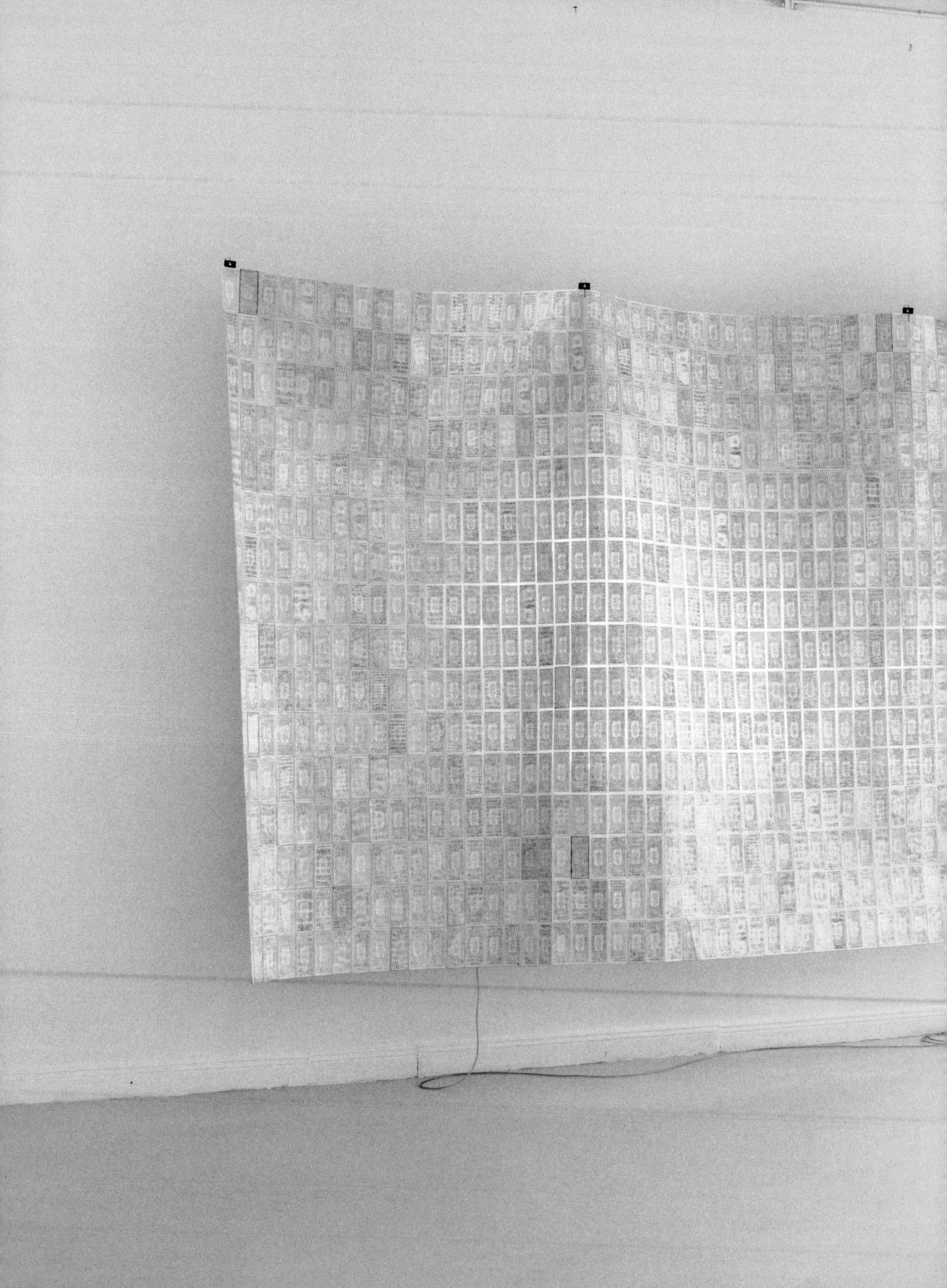

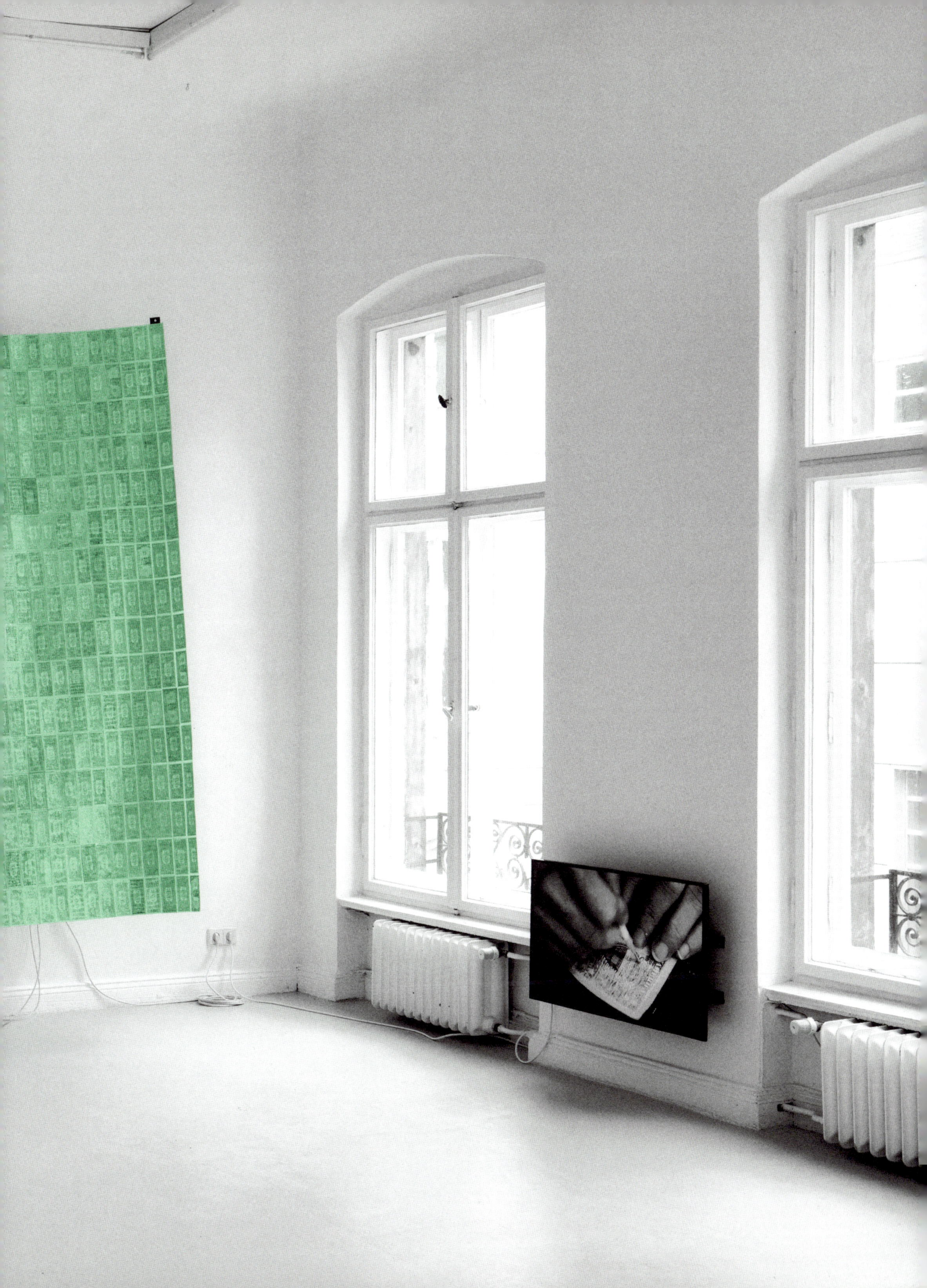

53 BEGINNINGS

 53 beginnings 2011 **12" vinyl** Siebdruckcover **silkscreen print cover, inlay**

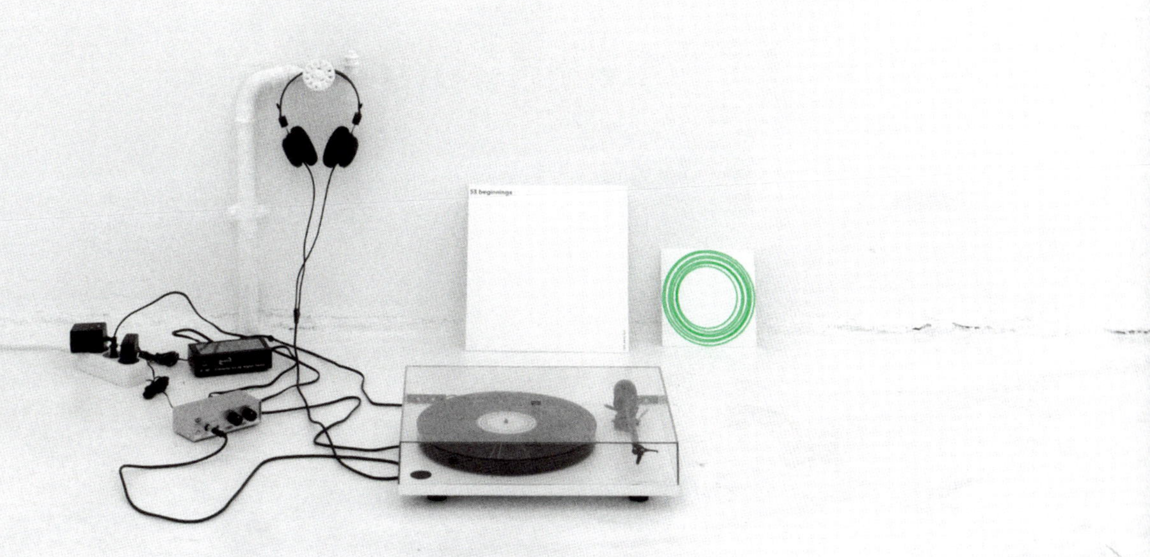

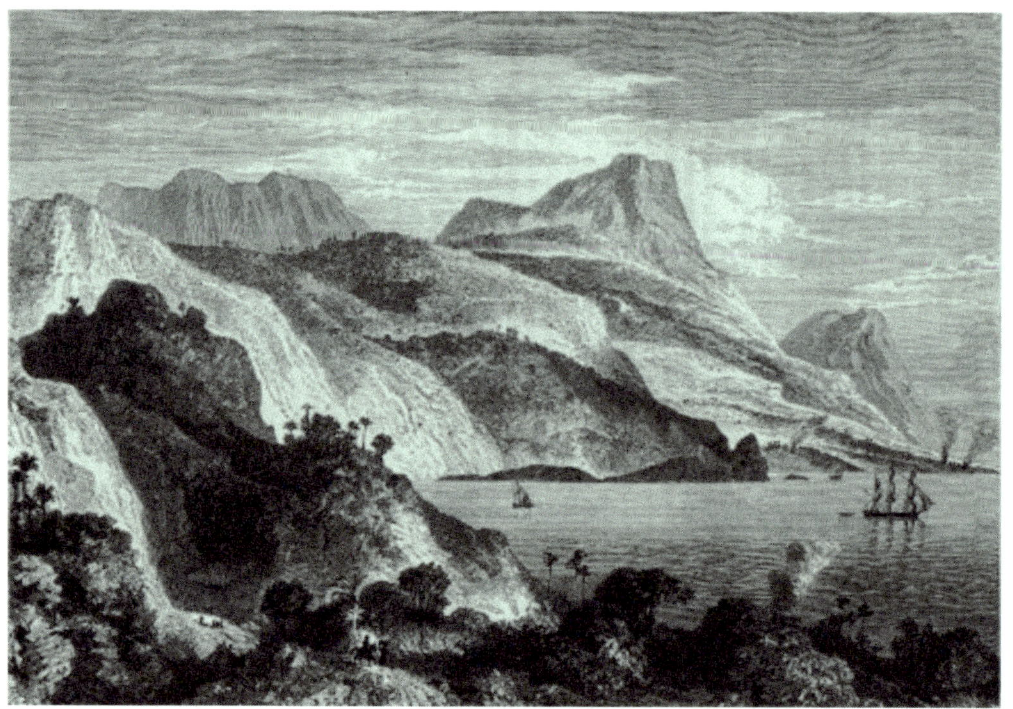

SIDE A: 1 MAX ROACH, WE INSIST, CANDID 1986 / 2 THE STYLE COUNCIL, THE PROMISED LAND (JOE SMOOTH'S ALTERNATIVE CLUB MIX), POLYDOR 1989 / 3 DAVID CROSBY, IF I COULD ONLY REMEMBER MY NAME, ATLANTIC 1971 / 4 THE FALL, EXTRICATE, COG SINISTER 1990 / 5 26 KARLHEINZ STOCKHAUSEN, GESANG DER JÜNGLINGE - KONTAKTE, DEUTSCHE GRAMMOPHON 1968 / 6 THE CLASH, SANDINISTA, CBS 1980 / 7 THE X-SEAMEN'S INSTUTUTE - SINGS AT THE SOUTH STREET SEAPORT, FOLKWAYS RECORDS 1973 / 8 KEN ARA, MOZART, DEUTSCHE GRAMMOPHON 1972 / 9 LINTON KWESI JOHNSON, BASS CULTURE, ISLAND RECORDS 1980 / 10 PIERRE HENRY, MICHEL COLOMBIER, LES JERKS ÉLECTRONIQUES DE LA MESSE POUR LE TEMPS PRÉSENT ET MUSIQUES CONCRÈTES DE PIERRE HENRY POUR MAURICE BÉJART, PHILIPS 1972 / 11 LOUISIANA CAJUN MUSIC VOL 2 THE EARLY 30'S, ARHOOLIE RECORDS 1971 / 12 PRINCE AND THE REVOLUTION, AROUND THE WORLD IN A DAY, PAISLEY PARK 1985 / 13 ART BLAKEY AND THE JAZZ MESSANGERS, HARD BOP, COLUMBIA 1980 / 14 THE HOUSEMARTINS, BUILD, GO! DISCS 1987 / 15 BIG YOUTH, SCREAMING TARGET, TROJAN RECORDS 1972 / 16 DIE NEUE MUSIK UND IHRE HISTORISCHEN VORAUSSETZUNGEN 1, OPUS MUSICUM, ARNO VOLK VERLAG 1974 / 17 CAPTAIN BEEFHEART, DOC AT THE RADAR STATION, VIRGIN 1980 / 18 CLIFTON CHENIER, LIVE (AT A FRENCH DANCE), ARHOOLIE RECORDS 1972 / 19 JELLY ROLL MORTON, PIANO SOLOS, RCA 1972 / 20 SONGS AND DANCES OF HAITI, ETHNIC FOLKWAYS LIBRARY 1952 / 21 MILES DAVIS, SKETCHES OF SPAIN, COLUMBIA 1960 / 22 LE TOBAGO STEEL BAND, POUR RECEVOIR VOS AMIS COMME A TRINIDAD CARAÏBE, EMI PATHÉ MARCONI / 23 CODONA, ECM 1979 / 24 52ND STREET VOLUME 1, ONYX RECORDS 1972 / 25 ALBERT AYLER, FABBRI EDITORI 1979 / 26 FRANZ JOSEF DEGENHARDT, SPIEL NICHT MIT DEN SCHMUDDELKINDERN, POLYDOR 1965

SIDE B: 27 DEAD KENNEDYS, BEDTIME FOR DEMOCRACY, ALTERNATIVE TENTACLES RECORDS 1986 / 28 BLUMFELD, VERBOTENE FRÜCHTE, CBS SONY 2006 / 29 AN ANTHOLOGY OF NORTH AMERICAN INDIAN & ESKIMO MUSIC, ETHNIC FOLKWAYS LIBRARY 1973 / 30 DIE NEUE MUSIK UND IHRE HISTORISCHEN VORAUSSETZUNGEN 2, OPUS MUSICUM, ARNO VOLK VERLAG 1974 / 31 SEBADOH, WEED FORESTIN, HOMESTEAD RECORDS 1990 / 32 DINOSAUR JR., JUST LIKE HEAVEN, NORMAL RECORDS 1989 / 33 FSK, CONTINENTAL BREAKFAST, EDIESTA RECORDS 1987 / 34 THE GO BETWEENS, STREETS OF YOUR TOWN, BEGGARS BANQUET 1988 / 35 THE FALL, THE WONDERFUL AND FRIGHTENING OF..., BEGGARS BANQUET 1984 / 36 UT, IN GUT'S HOUSE, BLAST FIRST 1987 / 37 ROBERT FORSTER, DANGER IN THE PAST, BEGGARS BANQUET 1990 / 38 FOLK AND CLASSICAL MUSIC OF KOREA, ETHNIC FOLKWAYS LIBRARY 1951 / 39 AUSTRALIAN FOLK SONGS AND BALLADS, FOLKWAYS RECORDS 1960 / 40 MIRIAM MAKEBA, THE MANY VOICES OF MIRIAM MAKEBA, KAPP RECORDS 1962 / 41 MOZART, STRING QUARTETS, SUPRAPHON 1985 / 42 SIBELIUS, SYMPHONIE 2 D-DUR, DEUTSCHE GRAMMOPHON 1969 / 43 OSCAR PETERSON CLARK TERRY, AMIGA 1976 / 44 VERDI, OTELLO, DECCA 1970 / 45 FOLK MUSIC OF JAMAICA, FOLKWAYS RECORDS 1956 / 46 MOONDOG, SNAKETIME SERIES, MOONDOG RECORDS 2007 / 47 DUKE ELLINGTON COUNT BASIE, FIRST TIME!, CBS 1961 / 48 ELLA FITZGERALD JOE PASS, TAKE LOVE EASY, PABLO RECORDS 1974 / 49 PIXIES, SURFER ROSA, 4AD 1988 / 50 CALLAS, DONIZETTI LUCIA DI LAMMERMOOR, EMI / 51 THE GOLDEN GATE QUARTET, COLUMBIA / 52 THE BLACK CARIBS OF HONDURAS, ETHNIC FOLKWAYS LIBRARY 1952 / 53 ATAHUALPA YUPANQUI, LE CHANT DU MONDE 1970

53 beginnings

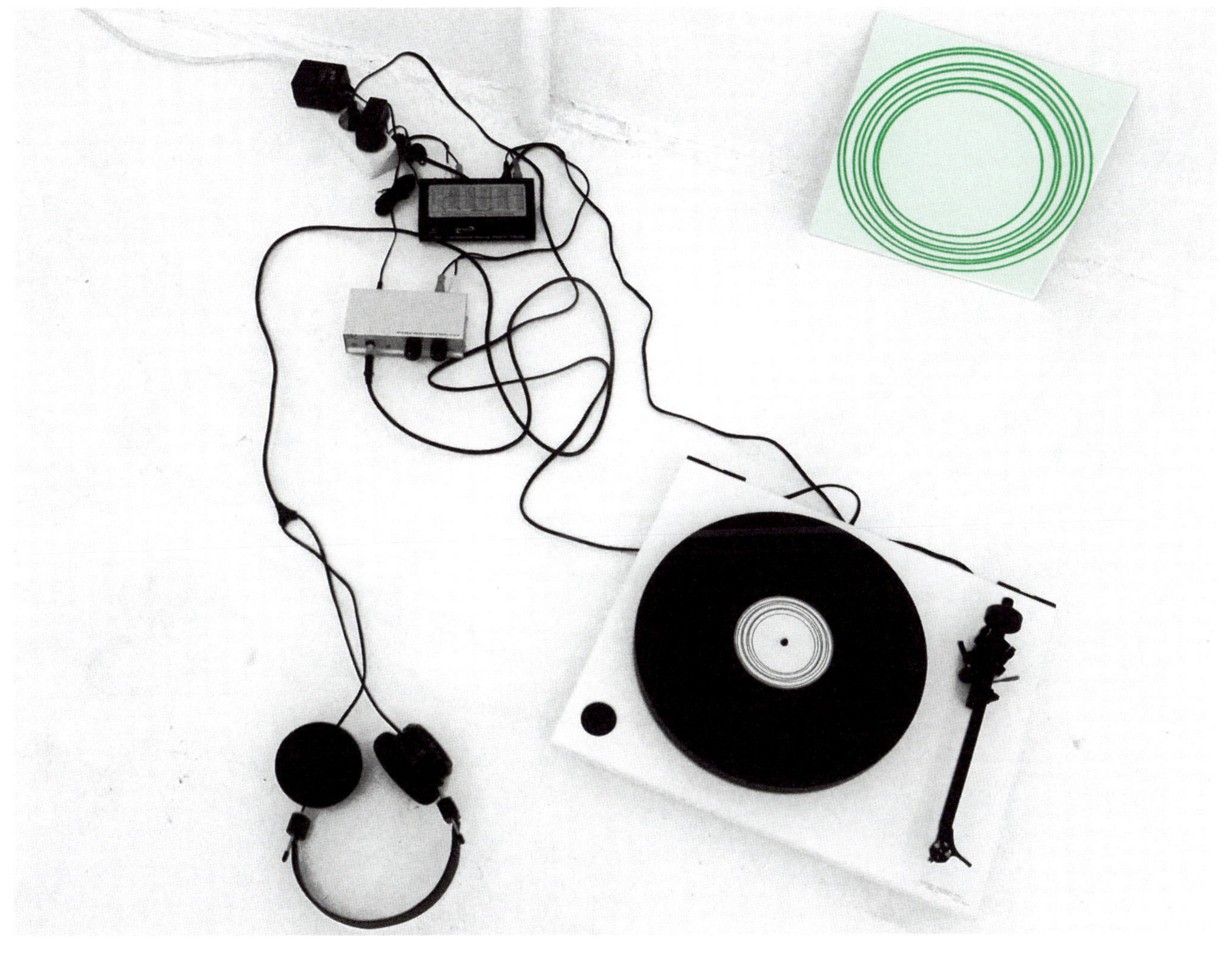

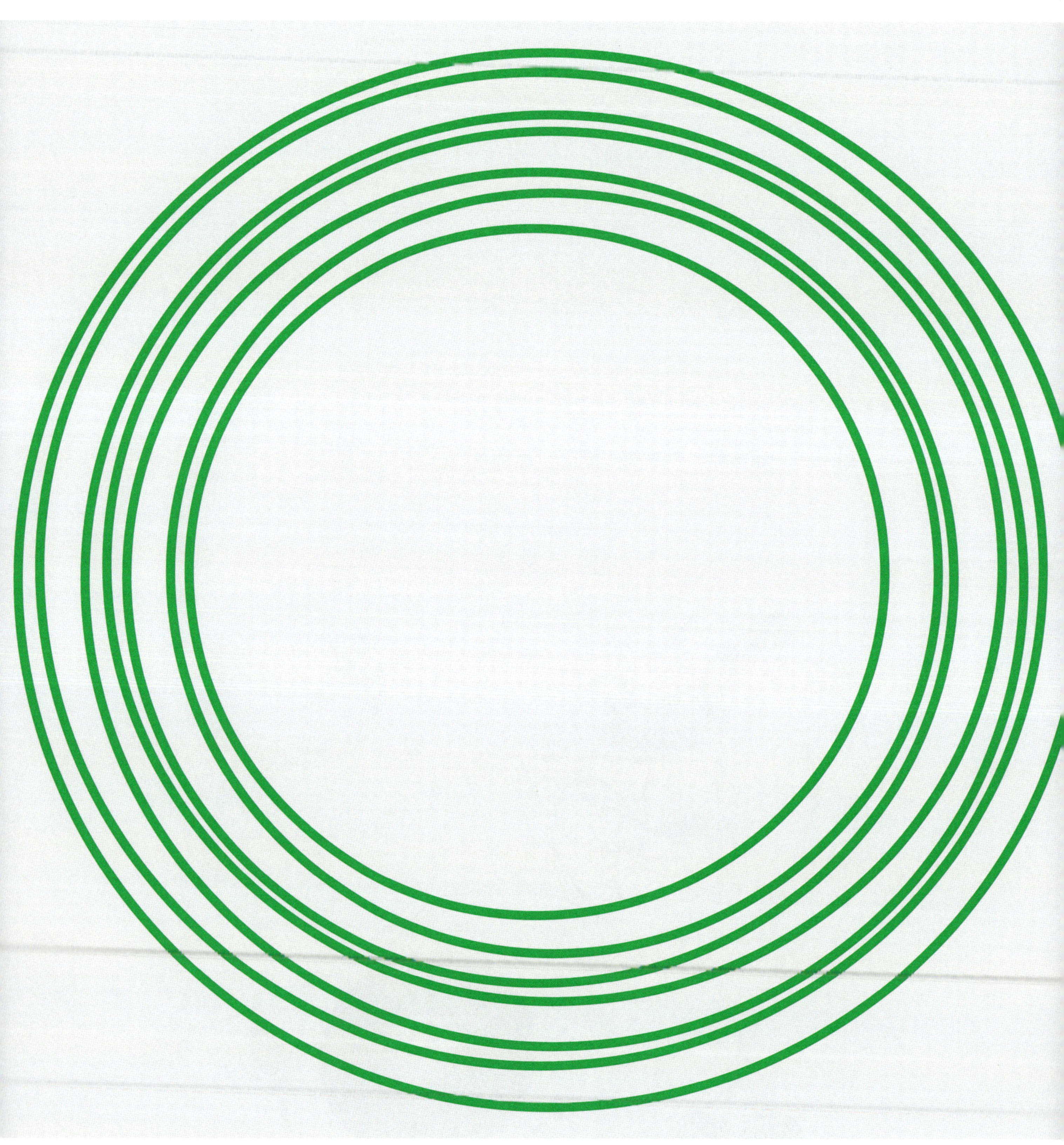

53 beginnings

53 beginnings

012012-1 33rpm NADINE FECHT

Biografien

Nadine Fecht wurde 1976 in Mannheim geboren und lebt und arbeitet in Berlin. Sie studierte Sprachen und Archäologische Zeichnung an der Humboldt Universität, Berlin (2000–2003) und schloss ihr Meisterschüler-Innenstudium in Bildender Kunst an der Universität der Künste Berlin 2009 ab. Seitdem wurden ihre Arbeiten u. a. in der Kunsthalle Mannheim (2019), im Kunstmuseum Basel, Schweiz (2017), MAC-UFPA Belém, Brasilien (2017), Museum für Konkrete Kunst, Ingolstadt (2017), Hamburger Kunsthalle (2016), Kupferstichkabinett, SMB Berlin (2013), Kunstverein Harburger Bahnhof, Hamburg (2013), Akademie der Künste Berlin (2013) ausgestellt. Sie hat verschiedene Stipendien erhalten, u. a. „Dorothea-Erxleben Programm" (2015–2017), Stiftung Kunstfonds (2013), „Berlin-Stipendium" Akademie der Künste Berlin (2012). 2014 wurde ihr der Will-Grohmann-Preis (Akademie der Künste Berlin) verliehen. Ihre Arbeiten sind Teil öffentlicher Sammlungen der Hamburger Kunsthalle (2012), der Berlinischen Galerie (2012/2013), dem Kupferstichkabinett Berlin (2013), dem Neuen Berliner Kunstverein n. b. k. (2014), dem Kunstmuseum Basel (2015) und dem Herzog Anton Ulrich-Museum Braunschweig (2018).

Von 2015 bis 2017 unterrichtete sie erweiterte Zeichnung als Lehrbeauftragte an der Hochschule für Bildende Künste Braunschweig und Zeichnung an der Schnittstelle zu Skulptur an der Universität Mozarteum in Salzburg. Von 2018–2019 verwaltet sie die Professur der Grundklasse Zeichnung an der HBK Braunschweig.

Thomas Köllhofer (*1960) arbeitet seit 1996 als wissenschaftlicher Mitarbeiter an der Kunsthalle Mannheim und seit 2000 als Leiter der Graphischen Sammlung. Er studierte Kunstgeschichte, Romanistik und Ethnologie in Berlin, Madrid und Freiburg.

Kolja Reichert ist Redakteur für Kunst im Feuilleton der Frankfurter Allgemeinen Sonntagszeitung. 2015 kuratierte er im Rahmen des Wiener Festivals „curated by" die Gruppenausstellung *Produktion* in der Galerie nächst St. Stephan. Preis für Kunstkritik der Deutschen Kunstvereine und der Art Cologne 2012, Will-Grohmann-Preis der Akademie der Künste Berlin 2018.

Krisztina Hunya arbeitet als kuratorische Assistenz am Neuen Berliner Kunstverein (n. b. k.) und ist Teilnehmerin der OFF Biennale Budapest 2020. Zu ihren letzten kuratorischen Projekten zählen das Symposium des f/stop Festivals Leipzig und *Ilona Németh: Eastern Sugar*, Kunsthalle Bratislava (beides 2018). Sie ist Absolventin des Masterstudiengangs Kulturen des Kuratorischen an der HGB Leipzig und erlangte ihren M.A. in Kunstgeschichte an der Freien Universität Berlin.

Biographies

Nadine Fecht **was born in Mannheim in 1976 and lives and works in Berlin. She studied languages and archaeological drawing at the Humboldt University, Berlin (2000–2003) and completed her masters in Visual Arts at the Berlin University of the Arts in 2009. Since then her work has been exhibited, amongst other places, at the Kunsthalle Mannheim (2019), the Kunstmuseum Basel, Switzerland (2017), MAC-UFPA Belém, Brazil (2017), Museum für Konkrete Kunst, Ingolstadt (2017), Hamburger Kunsthalle (2016), Kupferstichkabinett, SMB Berlin (2013), Kunstverein Harburger Bahnhof, Hamburg (2013), Akademie der Künste, Berlin (2013). She has received various stipends, including the "Dorothea-Erxleben Programm" (2015–2017), Stiftung Kunstfonds (2013), "Berlin-Stipendium" Akademie der Künste, Berlin (2012). In 2014 she was awarded the Will Grohmann Prize (Akademie der Künste, Berlin). Her work features in the public collections of the Hamburger Kunsthalle (2012), Berlinische Galerie (2012/2013), Kupferstichkabinett Berlin (2013), Neuer Berliner Kunstverein n. b. k. (2014), Kunstmuseum Basel (2015), and the Herzog Anton Ulrich-Museum Braunschweig (2018).**

From 2015 to 2017 she taught expanded drawing as assistant professor at the Braunschweig University of art and drawing at the interface to sculpture at the Mozarteum University Salzburg. From 2018–2019 she was substitute professor for the foundation class in drawing at the Braunschweig University of Art.

Thomas Köllhofer **(*1960) began work as a research assistant at the Kunsthalle Mannheim in 1996, and in 2000 was appointed Director of the Graphic Collection. He studied art history, Romance philology and ethnology in Berlin, Madrid, and Freiburg.**

Kolja Reichert **is an art editor for the Frankfurter Allgemeine Sonntagszeitung's feuilletons. In 2015 he curated the group exhibition *Produktion* at the Galerie nächst St. Stephan within the framework of the Wiener Festival "curated by". In 2012 he was awarded the art criticism prize of the Deutsche Kunstvereine and Art Cologne, and in 2018 the Will Grohmann Prize of the Akademie der Künste, Berlin.**

Krisztina Hunya **is curatorial assistant at Neuer Berliner Kunstverein (n. b. k.) and participant at OFF Biennale Budapest 2020. Among her recent curatorial projects were the symposium at f/stop Festival Leipzig and the exhibition *Ilona Németh: Eastern Sugar* at Kunsthalle Bratislava (both 2018). She holds an MA degree in Cultures of the Curatorial HGB Leipzig and in Art History, Freie Universität, Berlin.**

Bildunterschriften
Image captions

Titelblatt / Rückcover
Front / back cover
***Störungen sind Katastrophen* (Disturbances are Catastrophes) 2019,** Serie von Archivblättern, Mischtechnik auf Papier, Maße variabel **series of archive sheets, mixed technique on paper, dimensions variable**

6 ***mimikry (Amok)* 2017,** Letraset und Farbstift auf Papier **Letraset and colored pencil on paper, 41.9 × 59.2 cm**
9 aus **from: *Hitler,*** Peter Longerich, Siedler Verlag 2015
10 ***mimikry (Agency)* 2017,** Letraset und Farbstift auf Papier **Letraset and colored pencil on paper, 41.9 × 59.2 cm**
22 Studie zu *hysteria* **Study for *hysteria* 2016,** Tusche auf Papier **ink on paper, 29.7 × 21 cm**
22 ***hysteria* 2016,** Tusche auf Papier **ink on paper 210 × 950 cm,** fünfteilig **five-part**
23–27 ***hysteria* 2016,** Blatt **sheet 1, 2, 3, 4, 5** Tusche auf Papier, **ink on paper,** je **each 210 × 143 cm**
28 ***hysteria* (detail) 2016,** Blatt **sheet 2,** Tusche auf Papier **ink on paper, 210 × 143 cm**
30 ***Sensoren* (Sensors), Braunschweig University of Art, 2017,** (Ausstellungsansicht **exhibition view**)
32 ***mimikry (Selbstkritik)* [Mimicry (self-criticism)] 2017,** Letraset und Farbstift auf Papier **Letraset and colored pencil on paper, 41.9 × 59.2 cm**
34 ***privileged* 2016,** weiße Tusche und transparentes Klebeband auf Kohlepapier und Kohle auf Papier **white ink and transparent tape on carbon paper and carbon on paper, 278 × 545 cm,** Diptychon **diptych**
35 (oben) Studie zu **Study for *privileged* 2016, 42 × 29.7 cm**
35 (unten) ***privileged*** (Detail im Atelier **detail in the studio**)
36 ***privileged* 2016,** weiße Tusche und transparentes Klebeband auf Kohlepapier und Kohle auf Papier **white ink and transparent tape on carbon paper and carbon on paper, 278 × 545 cm**
38 ***privileged* (detail) 2016,** Kohle auf Papier **carbon on paper**
39 ***privileged* (detail) 2016,** weiße Tusche und transparentes Klebeband auf Kohlepapier **white ink and transparent tape on carbon paper**
40 ***privileged* (detail) 2016,** Kohle auf Papier **carbon on paper**
41 ***privileged* (detail) 2016,** weiße Tusche und transparentes Klebeband auf Kohlepapier **white ink and transparent tape on carbon paper**
42–63 ***AMOK* Kunsthalle Mannheim, 2019** (Austellungsansichten **exhibition views**)
64 Studie zu **Study for *Melancholia* 2015,** Tusche auf Papier **ink on paper, 29.7 × 21 cm**
65 ***Melancholia* (detail) 2015/16,** Tusche auf Papier **ink on paper**
66 ***Melancholia* (detail) 2015/16,** Tusche auf Papier **ink on paper**
68 ***Sensoren* (Sensors),** Hochschule für Bildende Künste Braunschweig **Braunschweig University of Art, 2017** (Ausstellungsansicht **exhibition view**)
71 ***close reading,*** (Studio für Elektroakustische Musik, Akademie der Künste Berlin **Studio for Electroacoustic Music, Academy of the Arts Berlin, 2013)** Sprecher **speakers** (im Uhrzeigersinn **clockwise**) Spanisch **Spanish (Noemi Argerich),** Deutsch **German (Mathias Greffrath),** Englisch **English (Harry-Ed Roland),** Französisch **French (Judith Lavagna)**
72 ***close reading,*** Wortliste der im Film besprochenen Neologismen **list of the neologisms discussed in the film**
73–75 ***close reading* 00:05:06, 00:05:12, 00:05:19; 00:11:30, 00:11:34, 00:11:36; 00:39:43, 00:39:53, 00:39:55**
76 ***Kultur:Stadt (Culture:City),* Akademie der Künste, 2013** (Ausstellungsansicht **exhibition view)**
78 ***mimikry (Mimikry)* 2017,** Letraset und Farbstift auf Papier **Letraset and colored pencil on paper, 41.9 × 59.2 cm**
85 ***Jedes Kollektiv braucht eine Richtung* (Any Collective Needs a Direction) 2013, 1805** Kugelschreiber auf Papier **ballpoint pens on paper, ca. 300 × 150 cm** (Sammlung Schering Stiftung im Kupferstichkabinett Berlin **Schering Stiftung Collection in the Kupferstichkabinett Berlin)**
86 ***Jedes Kollektiv braucht eine Richtung* (Any Collective Needs a Direction) 2013, 1805** Kugelschreiber auf Papier **ballpoint pens on paper, 240 × 150 cm**
88 ***System und Sinnlichkeit* (System and Sensuality), Staatliche Museen Berlin, Kupferstichkabinett, 2013** (Ausstellungsansicht **exhibition view**)
89 ***move – align – avoid.*** *Vom Schwarm als Prinzip und Phänomen,* **(On the Swarm as Principle and Phenomenon) Kunstverein Harburger Bahnhof, Hamburg, 2013** (Ausstellungsansicht **exhibition view**)
90–93 ***Jedes Kollektiv braucht eine Richtung* (Any Collective Needs a Direction) 2013,** Serie **series, 1805** Kugelschreiber auf Papier **ballpoint pens on paper,** je **each 100 × 70 cm** (Sammlung **Collection of the Kunstmuseum Basel**)
94 ***mimikry (Disziplin)* 2017,** Letraset und Farbstift auf Papier **Letraset and colored pencil on paper, 41.9 × 59.2 cm**
96 ***Die Bewegung* (Movement) 2019,** Serie **Series (1650** Kugelschreiber auf Papier **ballpoint pens on paper,** je **each 240 × 150 cm 11-part) HD videoloop, audio**
97 Making of ***Die Bewegung* (Movement)**
98–100 ***Die Bewegung* (Movement) 2019,** Blatt **sheet 1, 3,** sowie **details** von **of: 8, 9, 10, 11, 1650** Kugelschreiber auf Papier **ballpoint pens on paper, 240 × 150 cm**
101 ***Die Bewegung* (Movement) 2019, HD videoloop** (Ausschnitt **excerpt)**
102 ***AMOK* Kunsthalle Mannheim, 2019** (Ausstellungsansicht **exhibition view**)
105 ***affirmation app,*** Motivationsblätter für die Sprecher **motivation sheets for the speakers**
106 ***affirmation app,*** QR Code zum direkten Download via Smartphone **QR code for direct download via smartphone**
107 ***affirmation app,*** grafische Benutzeroberfläche **graphic user interface**
108 ***affirmation app,*** die Sprecher **the speakers: Saul Lopez Pereyra (Mexico), Tuğba Şimşek** (Türkei **Turkey**), **Yashar Mazidi (Iran), Izzat Iqbal Cheema (Pakistan) Pierre Kandi (Burundi), Sophia Baader** (Dänemark **Denmark**), **Leyko Yamaguchi (Japan), Bryan Ortega (USA), Neha J Thakar** (Indien **India**), **Mimi Schlueter** (Indonesien **Indonesia,** Indonesisch **Indonesian**), **Jimmy Nestor (Haiti), Christina, Avramidou** (Griechenland **Greece**), **Mona al-Masri** (Syrien **Syria**), **Charlotte Giacobbi,** (Frankreich **France**), **Alissa, Lillepea** (Estland **Estonia**), Zhengtao Li **(China), Elina Ije** (Lettland **Latvia**), Irvan Azhari Pane (Indonesien **Indonesia, Batak**), **Kodac Ko** (Südkorea **South Korea**), **Inga Beyers** (Südafrika **South Africa**), **Gila Epstein (Israel), Nina Trbojevic-Schlüter** (Kroatien, **Croatia**), **Ljubisa Ciric** (Serbien **Serbia**), **Serena Ferrario** (Italien **Italy**), **Firas El-Simrany** (Libanon **Lebanon**), **Maarten Bosboom** (Niederlande **Netherlands**), **Natalia Piroschik** (Ukraine **Ukraine**), **Nadine Fecht** (Deutschland **Germany**), **Alice Schneider** (Schweiz **Switzerland**), **Eugen Schilke** (Russland **Russia**), **Natraj Athreya** (Indien **India, Tamil**)
115 Sammlung gefundener Preisschilder **Collection of found price tags**
116 ***surplus* (detail) 2013/18,** gefundene Preisschilder auf Wand **found price tags on wall, 500 × 700 cm**
118 ***surplus* (detail) 2013/18,** gefundene Preisschilder auf Wand **found price tags on wall, 500 × 700 cm**
120 ***surplus* (detail) 2013/18,** gefundene Preisschilder auf Wand **found price tags on wall, 500 × 700 cm**
123 ***MONEY MADNESS* Reinbeckhallen Berlin, 2018** Ausstellungsansicht **exhibition view**
125 ***sweatshop,*** Beschaffung der Devisen **acquisition of the currency**
126 ***MONEY MADNESS* Reinbeckhallen Berlin, 2018** Ausstellungsansicht **exhibition view**
127 ***sweatshop* 2016, HD videoloop** Standbilder **stills**
129 ***subjectivity as a material to trade/ Subjektivität als Material zu handeln* 2014,** weiße Tusche auf gebrauchten 1 USD Banknoten **white ink on used 1 USD banknotes (detail)**
130 ***Dialogues* VDA Berlin, 2017** (Ausstellungsansicht **exhibition view**)
131 ***active textures – between text and textile* Xc Hua Galerie, Berlin, 2019** (Ausstellungsansicht **exhibition view**)
132 ***active textures – between text and textile* Xc Hua Galerie, Berlin, 2019** (Ausstellungsansicht **exhibition view**)
135 ***field recording* Fruehsorge Contemporary Drawings, Berlin, 2012** (Ausstellungsansicht **exhibition view**)
136 ***53 beginnings,*** Inlay **inlay**
137 ***field recording* Fruehsorge Contemporary Drawings, Berlin, 2012** (Ausstellungsansicht **exhibition view**)
138 ***53 beginnings,*** Cover Rückseite, Siebdruck auf Papier **rear of the cover silkscreen print on paper**
139 ***53 beginnings,*** Cover Vorderseite, Siebdruck auf Papier **front of the cover silkscreen print on paper**
142 ***mimikry (Ordnung)* [Mimicry (order)] 2017,** Letraset und Farbstift auf Papier **Letraset and colored pencil on paper, 41.9 × 59.2 cm**

Ond

hung

Impressum **Colophon**

Dieser Katalog erscheint anlässlich der Ausstellung Nadine Fecht *AMOK*, in der Kunsthalle Mannheim, 19. Juli – 13. Oktober 2019
This catalog is published on the occasion of the exhibition Nadine Fecht *AMOK*, in Kunsthalle Mannheim, 19.07.–13.10.2019

Herausgeber **Editor**
***Thomas Köllhofer,* Kunsthalle Mannheim**

Konzeption **Concept**
Nadine Fecht, Eric Wunder, Studio Pandan

Gestaltung **Design**
Studio Pandan – Ann Richter & Pia Christmann

Texte **Texts**
Inge Herold, Krisztina Hunya, Thomas Köllhofer, Kolja Reichert, Eric Wunder

Übersetzung **Translation**
Colin Shepherd

Lektorat **Copy Editing**
Nadine Fecht, Sabine Fischer, Thomas Köllhofer, Mathias Listl, Saskia Schallock

Korrektorat **Proof Reading**
DISTANZ Verlag

Fotonachweis **Photo Credits**
Joe Clark* (130); *Michael Pfisterer* (89); *Marcus Schneider* (85, 86, 116, 118, 120, 123, 131, 133, 135); *Frank Sperling* (30, 68, 65); *Anton Tripp Fotoarchiv Ruhr Museum* (9); *Eric Wunder* (9, 66, 80, 107); *Kathrin Schwab* (6, 10, 32, 36, 38–41, 43–62, 78, 94, 142); *Cine-Archives, FR, Pay Numrich, Wales News Service* (101)** Wir haben uns bemüht, sämtliche Rechteinhaber ausfindig zu machen. Sollte uns dies nicht in allen Fällen gelungen sein, so bitten wir diese, sich bei uns zu melden. Berechtigte Ansprüche werden selbstverständlich im Rahmen der üblichen Vereinbarungen abgegolten. Alle weiteren **all further: *Nadine Fecht

Lithografie **Image Editing**
Prints Professional (Jan Scheffler)

Audio mastering (Flexidisc)
Heiko Daniels

Gesamtherstellung **Printing and Binding**
DZA Druckerei zu Altenburg GmbH

Vertrieb **Distribution**
edel Germany GmbH
www.edel.com
international-books@edel.com

Erschienen im **Published by**
DISTANZ Verlag
www.distanz.de

ISBN 978-3-95476-295-8
Printed in Germany

Gefördert von **Supported by**

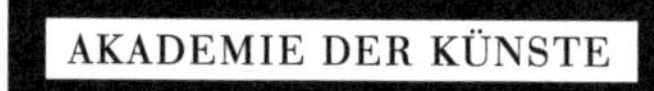

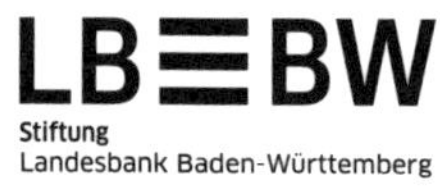

BILD-KUNST

MANNHEIM²

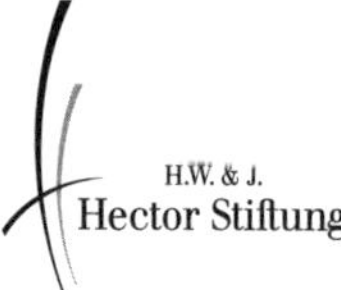

DISTANZ

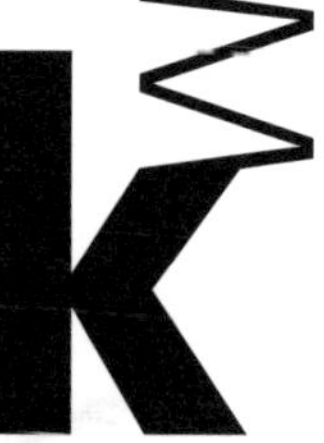